With Paintbrush & Shovel

LEOPARD'S-BANE

Arnica acaulis (Walt.) B.S.P.

With Paintbrush & Shovel

PRESERVING VIRGINIA'S WILDFLOWERS

Watercolors by Bessie Niemeyer Marshall

Nancy Kober

Donna M. E. Ware, *Botanical Consultant*

Published by the University Press of Virginia,
in association with the Petersburg Garden Club
Charlottesville and London

The University Press of Virginia
© 2000 by The Petersburg Garden Club
All rights reserved
Printed in China

Second printing 2001

♾ The paper used in this publication meets the minimum requirements
of the American National Standard for Information Sciences—Permanence
of Paper for Printed Library Materials, ANSI Z39.48-1984.

Library of Congress Cataloging-in-Publication Data
Marshall, Bessie Niemeyer.
    With paintbrush and shovel : preserving Virginia's wildflowers / watercolors by Bessie
Niemeyer Marshall ; Nancy Kober.
        p. cm.
    Includes bibliographical references.
    ISBN 0-8139-1969-X (cloth: alk. paper)
    1. Botanical illustration—Virginia. 2. Wild flowers—Catalogs and
collections—Virginia—Petersburg. 3. Lee Park Herbarium—Catalogs. I. Kober, Nancy.
II. Title.

QK98 .M327 2000
581.9755'0222'5—dc21
                                                                  99-089912

CONTENTS

ACKNOWLEDGMENTS

The Petersburg Garden Club, Nancy Kober, and Donna M. E. Ware are indebted to the many people and organizations who helped to make this book possible.

Our profound gratitude goes to Helen Marshall Fedziuk, the late Herbert Holden, and Helen Holden, who generously shared their family memories and materials and who showed enormous cooperation and patience throughout the process of putting together this book. We also extend special thanks to the following members of the Marshall family: Elizabeth Marshall Digges, Betty Harris, Katharine Fontaine Heath, Elizabeth Nash MacKenzie, Bruce M. Marshall, Gladys Fawcett Marshall, Isabelle Montgomery Marshall, Richard C. Marshall, and Louise Marshall McCrensky.

We owe considerable thanks to the following people who helped us to gain a better understanding of the lives and work of the women and men who played a role in creating the Lee Park Wildflower and Bird Sanctuary and the Lee Park Herbarium Collection: the late Mary Bell Focie, Percilla Anderson, Marion Anderson, Miriam Baughman, Garland Brockwell, Ray Daniels, Ann Jackson, the late J. B. Jackson, Frances Lunsford Johnson, Anne Lewis, Frank Myers, and Samuel Robinson.

We are most grateful to the Garden Club of Virginia, the Gwathmey Foundation, the Pamplin Foundation, and the Titmus Foundation for their contributions of funding.

Our deepest thanks are extended to Dorothy Caudle, who painstakingly photographed all 238 paintings in the Lee Park Herbarium

Collection and who contributed to this project in countless other ways. We also greatly appreciate the insights, advice, background materials, financial assistance, and other support provided by the following people, organizations, and businesses: James R. Baron, C. R. Berquist, Chris Calkins, Mary Calos, David Canada, Frank Carter, Richard Carwile, Martha Case, the staff of Centre Hill Mansion, Douglas Coleman, Susan Crawford, William Creech, Lucious Edwards, Gary P. Fleming, Harriet Frye, Carole Gallucci, Ray W. Garland, Judy Gilman, James W. Hardin, Boots Holden, Hal Horwitz, Gerald H. Johnson, Richard Jones, Clarence Joyner, Will Kerner, J. Christopher Ludwig, Nancy J. Martin-Perdue, Lawrence McLaughlin, Amy Meyers, Lou Musgrove, Merri Nelson, Karen Oliver, Owen Printing Company, Charles L. Perdue, Jr., the Petersburg Architectural Review Board, Pine Tree Press, Plummer Printing Company, Irene F. Preston, Joe Raucci, Timothy Richard, Camille Robinson, Joe Rountree, Bill D. Saunders, Suzanne Savery, Joe Schwartz, Stanwyn G. Shetler, Guthrie Smith, Thomas Smith, Sterling Press, Larry Toombs, Dulaney Ward, Stewart Ware, James White, Robert Whittet, Thomas F. Wieboldt, Robert A. S. Wright, and Stephen Wright.

Finally, the members of the Petersburg Garden Club convey their deep appreciation to Betty Steele, who envisioned the rebirth of a cause with commitment and dedication, and to Bettie Guthrie, who has been a vital collaborator in bringing this project to fruition.

An Uncommon Collection
Saved from Obscurity

Some Antique Scrapbooks Resurface

Among the many events organized in April 1969 to celebrate Historic
Garden Week in Virginia was a tour of the Georgian-style residence of
Joseph and Kay Prince of Petersburg. Visitors to the Prince home could
stroll across the expansive rear lawn edged with boxwoods ("No spike
heels, no smoking please!" the Garden Week program admonished).
Inside the house, they could pause in the elegant central hall, then
proceed to the dining room to admire a rare 1753 Sevres platter. In the
living room, the program promised, they could see "the Herbarium
that won the Massie Medal for the Petersburg Garden Club in 1948."[1]

This reference to a Petersburg herbarium in the Garden Week program must have seemed meager next to the more effusive descriptions
of Richmond estates and Charlottesville country gardens. Only those
who appreciated the prestige of the Massie Medal—an award given
annually by the Garden Club of Virginia for distinguished achievements
in gardening or effective protection, restoration, and preservation of
the natural beauties of Virginia—would have suspected that this particular herbarium was anything more than the typical collection of
pressed and dried plant specimens.

But the Lee Park Herbarium Collection was indeed something

more. Owned by the Petersburg Garden Club, it consisted of 325 pressed and dried specimens of Virginia wildflowers, accompanied by 238 watercolors of most of the same species.[2] The collection had been assembled during the 1930s and 1940s to document the wide variety of species that grew in a Petersburg wildflower sanctuary funded by the Works Progress Administration (WPA), the largest of the New Deal employment programs. The specimens had been taped to sturdy paper, covered with isinglass (a transparent film made from fish bladders), and compiled into albums. The companion watercolors had been mounted on opposite pages of the albums. The paintings were the work of Bessie Niemeyer Marshall, a local artist who had died in 1960 after receiving scant recognition for her work during her lifetime.

Only a portion of the collection's fourteen albums were on display in the Prince living room. The exhibit marked a rare appearance of the volumes outside their usual home—the Petersburg Public Library, where they had been placed in the 1930s so the whole community could enjoy and learn from them. By the late 1960s, few people remembered the collection or even knew it was there. Occasionally a browser might chance upon the volumes in the library stacks and page through their contents and perhaps wonder how and why they had come into being. But the artist and the project director and most of the people who knew the answers had died, and barely a trace remained of the wildflower sanctuary that had once occupied several acres of the city's Lee Memorial Park.

The pressed and dried specimens had their own subtle allure, but what most captivated the visitors that day in 1969 were the exquisitely detailed watercolors. Veins seemed to pop out from the undersides of leaves, tiny hairs bristled on dainty stems, and the chalky film on the dark berries looked real enough to rub off. The colors ranged from the diaphanous mauve of the lily-leaved twayblade to the vibrant orange of the turk's-cap lily. Here were dogwood and cat-tail, angelica and witch-hazel, Queen Anne's lace and prince's pine, huckleberry, dewberry, pokeweed, joe-pye weed, redbud, blue flag, and white

LEE PARK SANCTUARY—HERBARIUM
FLORA OF VIRGINIA

Scientific Name *LIRIODENDRON TULIPIFERA L.*
Common Name *TULIP TREE*
Locality *LEE PARK SANCTUARY, DINWIDDIE Co.*
Habitat *WOODS*
Collector *W.P.A. WORKER*
Date *MAY 2, 1939*

To create the Lee Park Herbarium Collection, Donald Holden and members of the Petersburg Garden Club pressed, dried, and mounted more than three hundred plant specimens, such as this one of tulip-tree (*Liriodendron tulipifera*). (Photograph by Will Kerner.)

fringed orchis. "I fell in love with those paintings," said Dorothy Caudle, a Petersburg woman who took the tour that day. "I had never seen anything quite like them. They were in old-fashioned scrapbooks tied with ribbon," she recalled, "and I was fascinated—the way they were drawn, the naturalness of them."[3]

This modest 1969 display was a small but crucial step toward the rediscovery of a small slice of Virginia history. Dorothy Caudle never forgot the watercolors. In 1989, she took her friend Betty Steele to see them at Richard Bland College, a junior college in Petersburg where they were then housed. Betty at that time was president of the Petersburg Garden Club, but like many club members she had never seen the collection. "I was so excited," said Betty. "I just thought the art was so beautiful. I really wanted us to do something with it."[4] With Betty's encouragement and with support from several other members, the Petersburg Garden Club, an affiliate of the Garden Club of Virginia, made plans to restore the aging collection and to learn more about the people who created it.

The story behind the herbarium collection turned out to be more complex than almost anyone realized. It is a story about art, botany, and social history, and about the lives of a diverse group of women, black and white, in a small southern city in the 1930s. At its center is a distinctive and little-known WPA project that operated in Petersburg from 1935 to 1940—a project designed to create jobs for women and to preserve native plants.

Both the Lee Park Wildflower and Bird Sanctuary and the Lee Park Herbarium Collection were products of a time that was harsh in many ways. Many Americans were out of work or just scraping by. Petersburg resident Samuel Robinson, who was a boy during the Great Depression, remembered pulling his little wagon downtown to the government relief center "to get that little bit of food they gave out, grapefruit, oranges—some of them were rotten—powdered milk and beans."[5] Job opportunities for women were limited, and those who did find jobs were paid less than men and encountered other work-place obstacles. African Americans had to deal with deeply entrenched patterns of segregation and discrimination in nearly every aspect of their lives.

But it was also a time when social change was shaking up the usual order, even in conservative states like Virginia. Government was assuming a more activist role in many arenas. Women employed through New Deal programs were demonstrating that they could handle non-traditional jobs. Communities were taking steps, often with government support, to preserve local history, protect the environment, and promote artistic expression. The herbarium collection was an outgrowth of all of these trends.

The History of the Herbarium Collection

From a botanical perspective, the Lee Park Herbarium Collection is significant because it is the primary surviving record of the species that grew in a particular place at a key point in Virginia's environmental history—a time when "the efficiency of bulldozers had not yet reached critical proportions," as the botanist A. M. Harvill observed in a journal article, and when botanists were just beginning to study many pristine habitats.[6]

The collection contains a fascinating diversity of wildflowers, flowering shrubs, and even some flowering trees—295 species, including many plants native to Virginia that captured the interest of colonial botanists in the seventeenth and eighteenth centuries. As the collection confirms, some fifteen rare or imperiled species grew in or near Lee Park in the 1930s—among them, the small whorled pogonia (*Isotria medeoloides*), an orchid that was considered rare even then and is currently on the federal list of threatened species. Also represented in the collection are several southern species near their northern limits in the eastern United States, and others near their eastern limits.[7]

From a historical standpoint, the collection is even more remarkable. Although herbaria are sometimes viewed as the elite province of botanical scholars and genteel hobbyists, this one was the populist byproduct of a Depression-era work-relief project. Many people in the community, including garden club volunteers, WPA supervisors and workers, a local artist, and others contributed time, expertise, or materials to develop the herbarium. But what really distinguishes the collection from other herbaria is its uncommon pairing of botanical art with botanical specimens.

A central figure behind the creation of the collection was an energetic woman named Donald Claiborne Holden, the director of the WPA sanctuary and a founding member of the Petersburg Garden Club. (Her first name was Mary, but she had always been called by her middle name, Donald.) Donald was a congenial yet somewhat formidable woman; at five feet eleven inches, she was always the tallest in any group of mothers, her son Herbert Holden recalled. As the daughter of a prominent Civil War surgeon, she was well established in Petersburg social circles, but her husband had died insolvent in the middle of the Depression, and she became the family's breadwinner.[8]

The Petersburg Garden Club, established in 1925, also played an instrumental role in developing the collection. The club was an original cosponsor of the Lee Park sanctuary and paid some of the costs of the herbarium collection. Club members helped to compile the collection and have maintained it ever since.

It is not clear whether Donald herself came up with the idea of making a herbarium of the park's flora, or whether it was suggested by someone else, perhaps a state WPA administrator. In any case, she seized on it with enthusiasm, refined the concept, and eventually promoted it among other WPA sanctuaries. Sometime in the winter of 1936–37, after the Lee Park sanctuary project had been underway for almost a year, Donald began to develop the herbarium. It would fulfill three purposes: education, documentation, and preservation. WPA workers, students, gardeners, and local citizens could study the dried specimens to learn more about various species of plants and their distinguishing characteristics. The herbarium would also serve as a running record of the species growing in the Lee Park sanctuary. And, as Donald explained in the *W.P.A. Record,* "some of the work that has been accomplished on this project will live on in future years."[9]

Donald asked the WPA workers and supervisors to bring her specimens of different plants from Lee Park and its environs, and once in a while she collected the specimens herself. She identified the specimens with help from the members of the Petersburg Garden Club and occasionally from the University of Richmond botanist Robert Smart. (It was Smart who confirmed her suspicion that the little plant with a long corolla was indeed *Polygala incarnata,* or pink milkwort.) Donald then pressed the flower specimens, sometimes using "these big old books my grandmother had, medical books, encyclopedias," Herbert Holden recalled. After the specimens were dried, garden club members mounted them.[10]

In early 1937, Donald devised a way to make the collection even better. She described her moment of inspiration in a piece written for a 1948 garden club meeting: "I had a difficult time classifying the plants for the herbarium. One day an idea was formed. I would have the wild plants painted in their natural colors, laying particular stress on their botanical points, then garden club members would know their names." It just so happened that the right person for this job—Bessie Niemeyer Marshall, an easy-going woman who loved wildflowers and had already demonstrated her talents in a series of life-sized floral paintings—was living across the street from Donald. Bessie was a newcomer to Petersburg who had accompanied her husband, an Episcopal minister, to a temporary rectorship. Like Donald, she was an enthusiastic gardener. Donald, a devout Christian, believed that it was more than chance that had brought Bessie to her neighborhood. "Mother used to say that the Lord had wanted Mrs. Marshall to do this, and had placed her right across the street," said Herbert.[11]

With funds from the WPA and later from the garden club, Donald commissioned Bessie in the spring of 1937 to paint the same species represented by the dried specimens, a task that would occupy the artist for the next three years. It was a welcome commission; Bessie's husband, disabled by Parkinson's disease, was about to retire, and the couple and their nine children would be making do on his limited pension. When Bessie completed a group of paintings, garden club members would mount them on backings and organize them, along-

A pressed and dried specimen of silky leather-flower (*Clematis ochroleuca*) in the fruiting stage, one of 325 specimens in the Lee Park Herbarium Collection. The original labels show when, where, and by whom the specimen was collected. (Photograph by Will Kerner.)

side their corresponding pressed specimens, into scrapbooks donated by the head librarian of the Petersburg Public Library. Within each scrapbook, the plants and paintings were grouped by their botanical families; when a volume was completed, it was placed in the library.

In 1940, WPA funding for the sanctuary project ran out, and Donald went on to other jobs. But in her mind, the herbarium collection was not yet complete. For several years, she had harbored the hope that someday the Petersburg Garden Club could win the Massie Medal of the Garden Club of Virginia. In 1933, she had seen a historic memorial oak tree in Norfolk; the woman who had preserved the tree, Mrs. Fergus Reid, had won the medal for this accomplishment. "I came back from that meeting [in Norfolk] with one thought in mind," Donald wrote; "how could our club win the Massie Medal?" When members of the Garden Club of Virginia toured the Lee Park sanctuary in 1940, Donald's thoughts again turned to the Massie Medal. In honor of the occasion, Bessie Marshall had painted a wildflower picture for the president of each visiting garden club. "The Herbarium was so complimented by everyone that saw it," wrote Donald, "that again, I wondered why we couldn't enter it for the Massie Medal."[12]

Donald had taken a leave from the Petersburg Garden Club soon after her husband died, but in 1946 she resumed active membership with the goal of preparing to enter the herbarium collection in competition for the Massie Medal. The club, with its own funds, commissioned Bessie Marshall to paint more watercolors to fill out the collection. In May 1948, Donald's dream was realized, and the Petersburg Garden Club won the Massie Medal. Eleanor C. Boothe, who chaired the Massie Medal committee, called the collection "one of the most outstanding pieces of work that I've ever known any club to accomplish" and marveled at how Bessie Marshall "has captured the soul of the flower in her work" and how "every detail of the flowers has been carefully preserved, scientifically classified and placed under isinglass and by some process the bloom of each flower has been elevated." The award was a high point in Donald's life; she wrote, "It was my faith in this work that kept my interest up these past fifteen years."[13]

Preserving the Collection

After winning the award, the herbarium collection went back to the public library, where it would stay for thirty-eight more years. Although never quite forgotten, the collection became a more distant priority as Donald Holden's contemporaries passed away and as new members joined the Petersburg Garden Club. Occasionally the club would do some maintenance work. Anne Lewis, a club member, remembered taking the volumes out of the library sometime in the late 1950s and working with others to reattach the loose specimens and paintings and "get the books into better shape."[14]

As time passed, the collection began to suffer the effects of age. Public library staff came and went, and concerns arose about the storage and security of the collection. Katharine Fontaine Heath, a niece of Bessie Marshall's, recalled going to the library in the early 1970s and asking to see it. "It was obscurely remembered," she said. "It was finally found. The pressed specimens were staining the paintings."[15]

In 1986, the Petersburg Garden Club moved the collection from the public library to Richard Bland College, a branch of the College of William and Mary. In this new location, the club felt, the collection would be more secure but could still serve an educational purpose. Over time, however, the club realized that it would have to take more aggressive steps to preserve the fragile collection and rehouse it under archival conditions. The paintings, which had seldom seen the light, had retained their color and clarity, but their backings and mounting adhesives had deteriorated considerably and had stained the paper. The specimens were mostly intact, but some of their backings had become dark and brittle.

In 1991, after consulting with preservationists, the club decided to move the collection to the museum at Centre Hill Mansion, a nineteenth-century house in Petersburg now open to the public. The club established a herbarium committee, chaired by Betty Steele, to oversee the collection's restoration and preservation; Bettie Guthrie later joined as co-chair. During the next several years, the committee members devoted considerable time, effort, and money to carrying out their charge and overcoming various obstacles, not the least of which was skepticism about whether a local garden club could successfully undertake this type of project.

After the move to Centre Hill, club members indexed the paintings and specimens and transferred them to acid-free storage materials. The herbarium committee enlisted Dr. Donna M. E. Ware, a vascular plant taxonomist, to evaluate the collection, check the identifications, and update the nomenclature. In the years that followed, the committee sought advice from experts in botanical art and restoration, researched aspects of the history of the collection, developed a photographic archive of all of the paintings, and organized exhibits of the paintings. The committee raised funds for its preservation work by selling limited-edition prints of Bessie Marshall's paintings, producing and selling stationery, writing grants, and other activities. Eventually, the committee arrived at the idea of a book as a way to bring Bessie Marshall's paintings to a wider audience and to tell the story behind the Lee Park Herbarium Collection and the WPA sanctuary.

The Petersburg Garden Club hopes to do additional restoration work on the paintings. The club has also launched an effort to preserve the wildflowers of Lee Park and to create an educational resource for the community in a dormant section of the park. This book is an important part of that preservation process.

Organization of This Book

The subject of this book is an unusual one with several facets, and it calls for a different approach from that of the traditional illustrated flower book or the typical history book. Although the text explores themes not usually found in a compilation of botanical illustrations—the Depression and women's work relief, to name just two—it does not aim to be a full historical account of the Lee Park sanctuary. Instead it tries to weave elements from art, botany, and women's history into a narrative that complements and enriches the illustrations.

The book is divided into two main parts. Part 1 contains the text, and part 2 presents the watercolors of Bessie Niemeyer Marshall. The chapters are organized by topic, rather than by strict chronology, so that readers can move as they like between the text and illustrations, focusing on topics that most interest them.

Part 1 consists of three chapters and an afterword. Chapter 1 sets the stage by describing the climate of the 1930s that led to the creation of the WPA sanctuary and the herbarium collection. It highlights three main trends: jobs for women, wildflower conservation, and community art and historical preservation. Chapter 2 gives a brief biography of the artist, Bessie Niemeyer Marshall, focusing mainly on her life during the 1930s and 1940s as she painted the Lee Park wildflowers and struggled to gain wider recognition. The story of the Lee Park WPA sanctuary and the women who helped to create it is set forth in chapter 3. The afterword moves out of the frame of the 1930s to describe present-day efforts to preserve wildflower habitats in Lee Park.

Part 2 contains reproductions of all but a few of the 238 watercolors Bessie Marshall painted for the herbarium collection. The paintings are arranged according to the habitats in which the plants grew in Lee Park.

PART ONE

The Story
of the
Lee Park
Herbarium
Collection

ONE

A Time of Social Change

Wildflowers and Work

In early December 1935, thirty-three women—twenty-six black and seven white—began clearing out dead branches and piling up compost along the wooded hills and steep ravines of a large city park in Petersburg, Virginia. Their goal was to establish a sanctuary that would preserve native flowers and birds in a region where several species of southern flora approached their northern limits and species of the mountains and Piedmont edged into the coastal plain. Supported mostly with federal funds from the Works Progress Administration, the sanctuary project created public jobs for unemployed female heads of households who could not find other work. But unlike the road, sewer, and school construction projects typically funded by the WPA, the Lee Park Wildflower and Bird Sanctuary was developed, directed, and built by women.

These women were working to support their families. Donald Claiborne Holden, the project supervisor, was a widow with five children. The WPA sanctuary job seemed tailor-made for Donald, a passionate horticulturist whose intricately designed garden was widely admired for its "Heinz plot" of fifty-seven varieties of iris. The WPA workers included women like Mary Bell Focie (then Mary Bell Goodwyn), a mother of three young sons for whom a WPA job relieved some of the pressure of supporting her family. "We worked for our children on the

WPA," she said in an interview decades later. "Thank God for the help I did get."[1]

From a statistical standpoint alone (and the WPA had an insatiable appetite for statistics), the women who worked on the sanctuary project during its five years of funding accomplished extraordinary things. Dressed in calf-length skirts and everyday shoes or galoshes, they cleared, dug, hauled, planted, mulched, and raked. By July 1939, the workers had transplanted into the sanctuary more than 365,000 plants —including 8,000 trees and 37,000 shrubs—from 1,500 acres of city-owned woodlands. They laid miles of pine-needle paths and labeled nearly 500 different kinds of plants with both common and botanical names. To retard erosion on fragile, fire-damaged stream banks, they reportedly planted 1,152,092 honeysuckle roots over a two-year period, an onerous task that took 7,980 person-hours and used 977½ bushels of leaf mold.[2]

The preserve these women created—a peaceful enclave that looked "deceptively natural," according to a feature in the local newspaper—drew tourists and gardeners from inside and outside Virginia. "We had right many folks coming in," said Ray Daniels, a Petersburg man who once worked as a guide at the sanctuary. "Back in those days, everyone was looking for something free to do, and this was free. The place had a good odor, too, especially after it rained."[3]

In a 1937 article for the *W.P.A. Record,* Donald Holden described what visitors to the Lee Park sanctuary might find: "What an adventure to explore the sphagnum bog and see and smell the fragrance of the laurel blooms, blue flags, orchids . . . and the pitcher and trumpet plants that gobble any insect so unwary as to explore their inviting interiors! The sundews are there too—those inconspicuous little plants that are carnivorous, their tiny red hairs reaching up and absorbing the meat that is placed above them. The banks of the shady little stream are planted with violets, rattlesnake-plantain, Indian pipes, ferns and various kinds of orchids, which makes a veritable paradise."[4]

Sixty years later, one must search carefully in Lee Park for clues

that a sanctuary ever existed—a few trails winding through the hills, some old wooden steps leading up a slope above Willcox Lake, the central feature of the park.[5] The signposts are long gone, as are the metal markers with the names of the plants, and it is hard to tell exactly where the sanctuary was situated. But the wildflowers still grow in Lee Park. In late April, a bulging lip of pink lady's-slipper pokes up from a mat of pine needles. In July, thickets of sweet pepper-bush perfume the air near the lake. In September, blue sprays of aster punctuate the open woods.

The women employed by the Lee Park project did more than create a tranquil natural area. They demonstrated that women could organize and carry out a major outdoor project. They also piloted a prototype

Women WPA workers transplanting flowers along one of the four main hills of the Lee Park Wildflower and Bird Sanctuary in Petersburg, c. 1937. (Courtesy of Tim Richard.)

for a federally funded wildflower conservation project that was later emulated by four WPA "sister sanctuaries" throughout the state, including one that eventually became the Norfolk Botanical Garden. And through the Lee Park Herbarium Collection, Donald Holden and Bessie Marshall developed a record of this conservation effort that would outlast the sanctuary itself.

Women and the New Deal

The sanctuary project and the herbarium collection were shaped by three broad trends that emerged during the early 1930s: the creation of New Deal work programs for women; a rising interest in wildflower conservation; and heightened attention to community art and historic preservation. While these trends may have been less dramatic in the relatively staid climate of Petersburg than they were in some other communities, they still produced some notable changes.

The Lee Park sanctuary, like other WPA projects, probably would not have happened had the economy been thriving in the 1930s. It took a serious economic upheaval to convince most Virginians to accept a stronger government role—even if just temporarily—in spheres that had never been thought of as government concerns. As part of this new government activism, a few forward-thinking leaders turned their attention to women's issues. Women in key positions in the Roosevelt administration sought to ensure that unemployed women received a share of New Deal funding and jobs; in the process, they hoped to change societal attitudes and break down some of the workplace barriers that women faced.

Although Virginia was not as hard hit by the Great Depression as some other states, Petersburg was one of the cities with "acute" unemployment, according to a 1932 state Department of Labor survey. The railroads were in a slump. Several textile manufacturers and a major tobacco company had closed down their Petersburg plants. Private charities could not keep up with the demands of thousands of unemployed, and the local Family Service Society expired altogether. Mary Bell Focie was one of many unemployed parents who had to scrounge to feed her family. Sometimes a friend would lend a hand with a donation of groceries, and other times she would wait in line downtown to get whatever donated food was available.[6]

For Mary Bell and thousands of other Petersburg residents, the enactment of the WPA in 1935 brought a welcome infusion of work-relief funds. With an initial national appropriation of $1.4 billion, the WPA was the largest federal domestic initiative the nation had ever seen. At the program's peak, some 3.5 million Americans—including 405,000 women—were employed in WPA jobs, which had to be publicly useful and performed on public property. To make the program more palatable in states like Virginia that were wary of federal control, the Roosevelt administration structured the program to give states and local sponsors some flexibility about which kinds of projects to support and how they would be carried out.[7]

With its WPA allotment, Petersburg put local people to work on a long list of public construction and improvement projects—roads, bridges, water mains, schools, recreation facilities, a city hall, and even a public golf course. But brick-and-mortar projects were not the only outcomes of the WPA in Petersburg and neighboring counties. WPA employees cooked hot lunches for schoolchildren, taught illiterate adults to read, painted murals in public buildings, controlled mosquito infestations, conducted oral-history interviews with former slaves, and started many social service programs still supported by the federal and state governments. During the month of August 1936, WPA projects in Petersburg employed 795 people, the majority of whom were black and almost half of whom (362) were women.[8]

What to do about women in need—single, married, widowed, or divorced women who were the primary wage earners for themselves or their families—was a much-debated issue within the New Deal. Determined women, not the least of whom was Eleanor Roosevelt, persuaded President Roosevelt to develop employment programs especially for women, first through the Federal Emergency Relief Administration and later through a Division of Women's and Professional Projects within the WPA. The head of the Women's Division in Washington, D.C., was Ellen Woodward, a gracious and politically astute woman from a comfortable Mississippi family who assumed increasingly demanding professional assignments after the death of her husband. Woodward was a forceful advocate of financial independence and equity for women—"I say frequently to the bride of this year or any other year, 'Go get a job,'" she told a reporter in 1938. Her efforts were buttressed at the state level by a dedicated network of progressive women like Ella Agnew, the state director of the WPA Women's Work Division in Richmond. Agnew was an effective and compassionate administrator who had been an educational missionary in South Africa, a YWCA administrator, and the first woman appointed by the U.S. Department of Agriculture to demonstrate food preservation and other skills to rural homemakers. She worked tirelessly to urge local relief directors to create jobs for women, a task she later described as "the most challenging work I had ever undertaken."[9]

Many local officials remained unconvinced that women could be the main breadwinners and refused to enroll them for work relief. When women did get federal relief jobs, local wage scales often locked them into lower rates of pay than men. In 1934, one advocate for women's rights wondered in a journal article why women with children employed in federal public works projects received thirty cents an hour for the same work that unmarried men were paid fifty cents an hour to do.[10]

The WPA women's division supported a wide range of projects employing skilled, semiskilled, and unskilled workers. In Petersburg, as in most communities, more than half the women employed by the WPA worked in sewing rooms, making bedding and clothing for indigent families. Others immunized children, typed and filed city records, mended library books, caned chair bottoms, staffed nurseries, canned vegetables, and kept house for the sick and disabled. Many of these projects were designed to employ women who lacked specific job skills or had limited educations but who were experienced in homemaking or farm labor.[11]

Landscaping was one type of activity proposed by Woodward and others to employ "unskilled" or undereducated women. As early as November 1933, the Emergency Relief Agency in Richmond suggested that women "may be valuable in landscaping public parks, playgrounds, open squares, school and court house yards and other publicly owned property." The landscaping projects attracted their share of critics, including many who considered outdoor work unsuitable for women. A county supervisor in Mississippi, for example, complained that raking was "too hard for women." By contrast, a woman administrator in North Carolina contended that many women were well accustomed to spending "weary days . . . plowing, chopping wood, scrubbing floors, dragging babies around, or bending over a wash tub for hours on end." Some communities created landscaping projects specifically as a way to employ black women with limited skills. On a national level, this practice drew fire from the NAACP, the black press, and others, who charged that black women were assigned to outdoor physical labor while similarly unskilled white women were sent to WPA sewing rooms—a criticism that would later be raised about the Lee Park project—and who rebuked some project sponsors for transporting women in open trucks during foul weather.[12]

Ella Agnew believed that women of all races were capable of doing outdoor work. In 1933, as legislative chair of the Virginia Home Economics Association, she wrote to Secretary of Labor Frances Perkins advocating "C.C. Camps for women," similar to the Civilian Conservation Corps camps that put young men to work protecting forests and preserving the countryside. This idea never took hold in Virginia, but when Agnew assumed her post in Richmond, she proposed another form of conservation work for women: creating wildflower and bird sanctuaries.[13] The Virginia sanctuaries were women's projects in their entirety. At the top levels of the WPA, Agnew and others provided funding, advice, and oversight. At the local level, women designed and administered the sanctuary projects and did the labor.

Petersburg was the first community to develop a WPA-funded wildflower sanctuary.[14] What motivated the city to apply for this type of project is not clear from the available records, but it does not seem to have stemmed from a desire to be a leader in women's advocacy. More likely the city sought to reduce its relatively high rate of unemployment among low-income women, particularly black women.

The Lee Park project brought together women of different races and backgrounds whose lives had been changed by the Depression in unexpected and mostly unwelcome ways. Their experiences on the job would be shaped more by their individual situations, and by the larger societal context, than by factors common to working women as a whole. For women like Donald Holden and Bessie Marshall—traditional, educated white southern women, who had been homemakers until they entered the workforce in middle age—the sanctuary and herbarium projects offered a chance to earn money, do interesting work, and gain new skills and confidence. For many of the black WPA laborers, like Lillian Anderson, the work could be physically exhausting, but the WPA paycheck of about eighteen dollars every two weeks could go a long way toward feeding her family, which then included seven children and would later include eleven.[15]

The women of the sanctuary did not see themselves as pioneers for women's rights. Nowhere in the reports of the Petersburg project or in the papers of the principal local figures are there discussions of women's changing roles or special challenges of working women. Although women in the higher levels of the WPA, like Woodward and Agnew, were thinking in these terms, issues of women's rights were remote abstractions for most local women. More typical of the local view was an observation from an article in the Petersburg *Progress-Index* about the impact of the WPA women's projects in the city: "Anything that will give 376 women a sense of security that comes from a pay envelope is not only worth while, it is a God-send."[16]

Preserving Wildflower Habitats

The Lee Park Wildflower and Bird Sanctuary took shape during a time of growing interest in native wildflowers and their conservation. During the 1920s and 1930s, Virginia botanists stepped up their efforts to locate and document occurrences of native plants, augment the commonwealth's herbaria, and publish papers for a wider audience. Groups like the Virginia Academy of Science, through its Committee on Virginia Flora and regional subgroups, encouraged botanists to make intensive surveys of local flora. In 1930, the academy published a field manual of regional wild flora, Paul Merriman's *The Flora of Richmond and Vicinity,* replete with descriptions of 700 species; Donald Holden was apparently one of its many lay users.[17]

Few botanists were as exuberant as the Richmond "orchid hounds." Their ranks included Jennie Jones, a feisty botanist with the Virginia Department of Agriculture, who did not let her wooden leg stop her from crisscrossing the hinterlands of southeastern Virginia in search of new colonies; and John Dunn, a Richmond oculist and intrepid orchidologist, who was known to venture out in the dead of winter in search of dried orchid seed pods. "I can still see his tall figure plunging down a steep railroad embankment, through the shifting cinders . . . or ploughing through the mud and slime of the James, recently overflowed," wrote botanist Clarence Williams of his friend Dunn. By 1935, Jones and Dunn had already documented several species of rare orchids in the Petersburg area, including white fringed orchis, spreading pogonia, and rose pogonia.[18]

Local interest in wildflowers intensified with the arrival of out-of-state botanists to prime haunts that had been closely guarded secrets among Virginia botany buffs. M. L. Fernald, director of the Gray Herbarium at Harvard University, spent fourteen seasons botanizing in southeastern Virginia, in quest of southern species for his eighth edition of *Gray's Manual of Botany.* Often accompanied by Philadelphia botanist Bayard Long, Fernald gathered specimens in such diverse

Petersburg-area locations as the freight yards, the Appomattox bottomlands, and the Poo Run bog, where a magnificent colony of trumpets thrived. With a field-press on Long's back and a hand-pick and vasculum in Fernald's tow, the pair cut curious figures as they poked around the rural backwaters. The regional rivalry escalated as Virginia specimens began to enrich the herbaria of northeastern institutions, a development noted by Edgar T. Wherry, a U.S. Department of Agriculture biologist, in a 1930 letter to Jennie Jones: "Dr. Dunn . . . mentioned that you had been inclined not to finish up your article upon this orchid [small whorled pogonia], because so many localities now seem to be known. I hope you will reconsider this, and go ahead and send the article to Rhodora, because it ought to be made plain to botanists that New England isn't the whole of the United States, and that the south has a few things to show the north."[19]

All of this activity brought home the realization that some native species and precious habitats were already disappearing. "[M]any of our former abundant plants are in danger of complete extermination," lamented preservationist Evie Bromley Key in 1939, in the journal *Claytonia*. She cited grazing, logging, forest burning, and real estate development as the main culprits and unleashed particular scorn on vandals and pirates. "Dealers have sent to the woods to bring in many of our loveliest flowers and plants," she wrote. "They do not realize the havoc they are wreaking and pull them ruthlessly out by the roots and so needlessly destroy them."[20]

In the mid-1930s, conservation-minded groups sought to remedy these problems by recommending the establishment of wildflower sanctuaries and by promoting wildflower preservation through articles, lectures, school visits, and exhibits. Local governments and civic organizations initiated sanctuary projects with public and private funds. Among the most active groups were garden clubs. By 1939, garden clubs were sponsoring at least fourteen wildflower sanctuaries throughout Virginia, including five supported with WPA funds.[21]

Lee Memorial Park in Petersburg was a prime choice for a sanctuary. A densely wooded expanse on the southern edge of the city, this municipal park was rich in both wildflowers and history. "Almost every locality has its own natural beauty, and Lee Park . . . is our special pride," wrote Donald Holden in a 1937 magazine article.[22] With hills, ravines, a deep valley, and an upland plateau, the park had a pleasantly rugged terrain compared with the downtown flatlands. It lay within the watershed of a stream called Willcox Branch, and it offered a variety of hospitable wildflower habitats, including lake margins, stream heads, fields, forests, and roadsides.

In fact, the entire Petersburg area, sitting almost astride two geological and floristic zones, was a robust botanical meeting ground where several southeastern species approached their distributional limits. This advantageous location proved a boon to the early naturalists who did fieldwork in Virginia. Plants, seeds, cuttings, descriptions, and drawings from the Petersburg area made their way to Europe's great herbaria and gardens and advanced the state of botanical scholarship. This history was a source of pride to Donald Holden, who boasted in a 1937 article that "the lore of the wild flowers of the Petersburg vicinity goes back more than 250 years."[23]

Three colonial botanists had particularly close ties to Petersburg and may well have tramped the lands that became Lee Park. The first, the Reverend John Banister (1650–1692), owned an estate about eight miles south of Petersburg and had ties by marriage to the Lee Park lands.[24] Banister documented more than 150 species of native plants and trees, and scholars at his native Oxford used his research to inform major botanical reference works.[25] The second, John Clayton (1693–1773), compiled an extensive catalogue of native Virginia plants, which he sent to Friedrich Gronovius, an eminent Dutch naturalist. Gronovius added some descriptions of his own, and in 1739 he published the work without Clayton's permission under the title *Flora Virginica,* listing himself as author but citing Clayton's contributions in a flattering introduction. Clayton did fieldwork near the north side of the Appomattox River and may have reached the southern banks near Petersburg; some botanists have speculated that a Clayton specimen of the spreading pogonia, a rare orchid, came from the Poo Run bog.[26] The third early botanist, physician James Greenway (1703–1793), lived some twenty miles from Petersburg in Dinwiddie County. He compiled a flora of Virginia plants which, although never published, won the admiration of Carolus Linnaeus and other acclaimed botanists.[27] Donald Holden's father had some of Greenway's medical books in his library.

Nearly a century and a half after Greenway's death, the lands around Lee Park were still relatively undeveloped—in part because of the Civil War. For much of that time, the lands remained in private hands and saw little activity, save some timbering and farming. With the onset of the Civil War, the Confederate army built a series of defensive earthworks along the contours above Willcox Branch, forming a segment of the famed Dimmock Line surrounding Petersburg. In 1864, during the siege of Petersburg, Confederate troops took advantage of the steep Willcox ravines to cloak their forays toward the Union flanks.[28] After the war, the presence of these historic breastworks helped to protect the adjacent lands from development for several decades.[29]

In 1893, the city of Petersburg bought 1,700 acres of private farmland, including the Willcox Branch watershed, to supplement its inadequate water supply. The city built a dam on Willcox Branch, creating a reservoir that came to be known as Willcox Lake. In 1921, the city annexed this tract, increasing the municipality's total land area by a third and bringing in new tax revenues from an affluent subdivision east of the lake.[30] That same year, the city council designated a 462-acre section of the annexation, including the breastworks, as a "great natural park" named after General Robert E. Lee.[31]

During the 1920s, the city constructed four and a half miles of road in Lee Park, using gravel from the park's own gravel beds. The city also built three miles of trails and sectioned off one end of the lake for swimming. (By this time the city was no longer using the reservoir

Willcox Lake, as seen from within the Lee Park sanctuary, 1939. (The Library of Virginia.)

for its water source.) The city installed a bathing pavilion, walking trails, baseball diamonds, picnic tables, and other recreational facilities. By the 1930s, the park was a popular and picturesque recreational site. But its pleasures were not equally available to all residents. City recreation facilities at that time were segregated, and the park's amenities, including the popular Willcox Lake swimming site, were off limits to black citizens. "You'd come by and see the swimming area and the picnic tables with all the food, but you could just look, and then you'd have to keep on going," said Samuel Robinson, a local black minister who used to walk through the park as a child. "If you were wandering around too much, the guards would put you out."[32]

When the WPA women began their work in Lee Park, they found many of the same species catalogued by Banister, Clayton, and Greenway—Indian cucumber-root, trailing arbutus, and laurel-magnolia, to name just a few. By all accounts, Donald Holden took the preservation aspects of her mission quite seriously, sometimes referring to the sanctuary as "this great work of conservation."[33] Although transplantation and some of the other strategies used in the WPA sanctuaries are no longer recommended, the Lee Park project would still accomplish several of its preservation goals. In addition, it would show how a partnership among federal and municipal government, civic groups, and businesses could further conservation in a community.

Community Art and Historic Preservation

The development of the Lee Park Herbarium Collection brought a New Deal populist spirit to the centuries-old botanical traditions of collecting herbarium specimens and producing botanical illustrations. In 1932, the Committee on the Flora of Richmond and Vicinity called upon professional botanists and interested amateurs to gather herbarium specimens to document the species occurring within a hundred-mile radius of Richmond.[34] Donald Holden may well have been aware of the committee's recommendation when she embarked on the plan to create a herbarium of the Lee Park wildflowers. It was an ambitious goal for someone who was not a botanist, and its success would ultimately depend on the involvement of many people. In this respect, the Lee Park herbarium project represented the kind of collective community action espoused by New Deal theorists—although the women involved no doubt took a much more pragmatic view of what they were doing.

Donald's idea to commission botanical watercolors to go along with the specimens was a particularly bold undertaking for a local project.

Although the practice of documenting plants through botanical illustration has a venerable history, it can be much more time-consuming and costly than collecting specimens, which is why botanical illustrations were so often sponsored by institutions or wealthy patrons. Donald must have appreciated how much more evocative the collection would be with the addition of the paintings. Her choice of Bessie Marshall to do this work reflected a long tradition of women artists' taking on botanical subjects.

The notion of producing botanical art as a reference tool for the community was also in keeping with the philosophy of "art for the millions" advocated by the Federal Art Project.[35] Begun in 1935, this nationally administered WPA project gave jobs to unemployed artists to create murals and sculptures for public buildings and to produce other works of art that would benefit their communities. The idea was to democratize the visual arts, so that they were no longer considered just the province of an urban elite. The Federal Art Project also helped to establish community art centers, located mostly in rural communities, where local artists could exhibit their work and community members could take art classes and attend lectures. Through the Index of American Design, the Federal Art Project employed graphic artists to make meticulous illustrations of American decorative and folk-art objects—and, in the process, to discover and document authentic American material culture.[36] Although Bessie Marshall apparently was not involved with the Federal Art Project, its existence may well have stimulated WPA administrators, including Donald Holden, to think about ways to integrate art into community life.

Another group of New Deal programs was awakening interest in historic documentation and preservation, a trend that also may have influenced the development of the Lee Park herbarium. A documentary unit of the Farm Security Administration produced photographs chronicling aspects of American culture. The New Deal publicity directors also encouraged local WPA projects to photograph the products of their labors, whether a giant new dam or an oak-splint basket.

In many Virginia communities, WPA funds supported local projects to inventory historic sites, restore old buildings, showcase indigenous handicrafts, and gather oral histories. Private organizations for historic preservation also came into their own during the 1930s. In Petersburg, the Association for the Preservation of Petersburg Antiquities was established, and renovations were begun on the Trapezium House, a nineteenth-century structure best known for its absence of right angles. Some fifty miles away, the restoration of Colonial Williamsburg was in progress.

Both the herbarium collection and the WPA sanctuary project used some fresh approaches to achieve what was in many respects a very traditional goal—preserving the commonwealth's heritage. This interaction between new and old ideas is a theme that would figure in several different aspects of these two unusual projects.

TWO

Bessie Niemeyer Marshall

Painting on the Porch

Bessie Niemeyer Marshall painted most of her wildflower watercolors at a green square table on her side porch. Here, on the west-facing side of a modest old house at 227 St. Andrew Street in Petersburg, she laid out her brushes, paper, and paints. A jug of water held her subject of the day—a spathe of skunk-cabbage or a bouquet of bird's-foot violets. On a cracked china saucer that served as her palette, she mixed her colors carefully, sometimes squeezing in the juice of a berry. Then she went to work, often for hours at a time, stopping occasionally to look in on her husband or chide her grandson and his playmates. "She'd struggle through the day putting up with us and trying to paint," recalled Garland Brockwell, a friend of her grandson's. "She had three rules: 'Don't kick up dirt, don't fight, and stay out of my garden.'"[1]

A soft-spoken, unpretentious woman who favored plain shirtwaist dresses, Bessie Marshall attracted little attention as she painted wildflowers on her porch, day after day. But taking shape at her table was a collection remarkable for its breadth, loveliness, and botanical precision.

Bessie had no formal training as an artist and could be modest, even dismissive, when discussing her talent. "An editor at *National Geographic* asked me what my school of art was, and I replied 'Miss Loretta Toomer,'" she said in a 1951 interview, referring to the few drawing and painting lessons she took as a girl at the home of a local Portsmouth woman. "As for the scientific accuracy the flowers are said to display," she added, "that came about purely by fluke."[2] Beneath this humility, however, was an inner confidence that appears to have sustained her as she attempted, in her fifties, to establish a career as an artist.

At the time Bessie Marshall was painting the Lee Park watercolors, she was also looking after children and grandchildren, taking care of a husband who was becoming increasingly disabled, and worrying about how to make ends meet. She shouldered these responsibilities with a sense of humor and an unflappable attitude. "I remember what a strong woman she was," said J. B. Jackson, a Petersburg friend of the Marshall boys. "I had the idea that she could do anything."[3]

Early Life

Born on Christmas Day, December 25, 1884, in the Swimming Point section of Portsmouth, Sarah Elizabeth Niemeyer was the second child of Hermann Christian and Louise Niemeyer (née Marie Louise Hook). Named after Sarah Howard Chandler Niemeyer, an influential grandmother with a sharp intellect, Sarah Elizabeth became "Bessie" at an early age, and so she remained.

Bessie had four sisters—Louise, Henrietta, Helen, and Margaret —and the Niemeyers' cozy home was often close to overflowing with relatives and visitors. Bessie was a well-mannered, good-natured child, with blue eyes, dark hair, and small hands and feet. As a young girl, she plunged into ambitious craft and sewing projects and spent much of her time perfecting drawings of Gibson Girls. The Niemeyers also encouraged their daughters to read books and memorize poetry.[4]

Hermann Niemeyer died when Bessie was fifteen. Although money was tight after that, the family maintained an active social schedule. Bessie played tennis, danced at the Chamberlin Hotel, and rode the train to Virginia Beach to attend house parties.[5] After graduating from high school, Bessie briefly taught school. She began dating Myron

Barraud Marshall, a tall, slim student at the Virginia Episcopal Seminary who also came from Portsmouth and was two years older than she. A great-great grandson of Chief Justice John Marshall, Myron was a scholarly man who had attended the Virginia Military Institute, then decided to enter the ministry. Myron and Bessie married on July 2, 1907, a month after Myron graduated from the seminary, and Bessie set up housekeeping with an ample trousseau of linens and clothing that she and her sisters had sewn. One striking example of Bessie's craftsmanship was a gift she made for Myron: a box for his starched collars, on which she had painted scenes of the happy events of their courtship. Myron always kept it on his bureau. His gift to her was a jeweled pin shaped like a pansy, which Bessie wore in a formal photograph taken when she was a young woman.

Bessie Niemeyer Marshall in 1909, age twenty-five. (Courtesy of Helen Marshall Fedziuk.)

Motherhood

Much of Bessie's adult life was devoted to raising children. The Reverend Mr. Marshall began his ministry in Saltville, Virginia, and there Bessie gave birth in 1908 to Louise, the couple's first child. Not long afterward, Myron took a missionary post in Zamboanga, Philippine Islands; in 1909 another child, Elizabeth (called Bits), was born. The baby was sickly, and the couple decided it was best for Bessie and the two children to return to Portsmouth. They moved back into the Niemeyer home, and a year or so later, Myron joined them.

In 1911, Mr. Marshall was appointed to lead a new Episcopal church, St. Andrew's, in the Ghent section of Norfolk. There the family lived for the next fifteen years, and there Bessie gave birth to seven more children: Catherine, Myron Jr. (called Son), Herman, Richard, Helen, John (called Bus), and Arthur (called Pinky), born in 1924. The large family put a strain on the minister's income. In 1926, he

Bessie and Myron Marshall and their nine children, c. 1926. Back row, left to right: Elizabeth (Bits), Catherine, Bessie, Myron, Louise. Front row, left to right: Helen, Arthur (Pinky), John (Bus), Myron Jr. (Son), Richard, Herman. (Courtesy of Helen Marshall Fedziuk.)

took a leave from the church to try to make money in the real estate boom in Florida, but he came back within a year. In 1927, he accepted the rectorship of St. John's Church in Halifax, Virginia, where the family lived for the next ten years.

Family and household duties occupied Bessie during the Norfolk and Halifax years, but despite these demands, "I never heard Aunt Bessie complain or say, 'I'm too busy,'" recalled her niece Katharine Fontaine Heath. The Marshall children were rambunctious, and Myron tried to keep order with strict times for homework and meals, a ten o'clock curfew on certain nights, and limits on the children's Sunday activities—rules that it sometimes fell to Bessie to enforce. Before breakfast and after dinner, the family had prayers and Bible reading, and Bessie also participated in women's circles and other church projects. On Sundays, the whole Marshall clan filled the second and third pews, right beneath the pulpit from which their father preached. The family also enjoyed cards, movies, and trips to the beach.[6]

Myron Marshall valued education and was determined that his children would attend college; all of them did, and seven graduated. (Arthur, the youngest, gained some fame as the inventor of VASCAR, a speed-tracking system used by highway patrols.) Bessie also loved books and had a talent for reading aloud and telling stories. On hot summer days, one might find a half dozen neighborhood children sprawled out in the Marshall living room, listening to Bessie read a Hans Christian Andersen fairy tale or a chapter from *David Copperfield*. "I recall sitting at her feet and asking for more stories until my parents reminded me for the umpteenth time that it was bedtime," her grandson Bruce Marshall reminisced.[7]

Crafts and Painting

Although Bessie seldom painted during her child-rearing years, she found other outlets for her artistic skills. She sewed most of her family's clothes—the girls' dresses even had matching underpants. For Christmas one year she made her daughter Helen a small cedar chest filled with handmade doll clothes that matched Helen's own dresses. For her niece Betsy she made twin paper dolls and a cardboard dollhouse with a nursery, a sunporch, a garage, doors that opened, and miniature furniture.[8]

In the early years of the Great Depression, Bessie entered a contest sponsored by a mail-order company to plan a home decor with furnishings from its catalogue. She constructed a three-dimensional cardboard house filled with tiny accessories she had made based on pictures in the catalogue. "I can see her twisting the rugs, making the lamps, wallpaper, draperies, the whole thing," said Helen Marshall Fedziuk.[9] After hearing nothing, Bessie finally contacted the company and learned that the package had been mangled in transit; the judges had failed to recognize it as an entry for the decorating contest.

By the time the Marshalls settled in Halifax, the younger children were growing up and the two oldest had gone off to college, giving Bessie some time to paint. She began accepting commissions for decorative painting on lampshades, card tables, and china. For her lampshades, she would paint a flower or bird design on the inside of the shade, building depth with layers of paint and adding details like the spots on a peacock's tail. When the lamp was turned on, the picture would shine through. Eventually the children became used to their mother painting between household chores. "We thought painting was just something mothers did," said Bits.[10]

In Halifax, Bessie also painted life-sized watercolors of dogwood, crepe myrtle, magnolia, morning-glory, althea, and petunias—some of her best work, according to her family. Somehow these paintings came to the attention of John Stewart Bryan, the president of the College of William and Mary. Bryan liked them and thought there might be a place to display them in Colonial Williamsburg. Bessie sent Bryan these paintings in a cardboard package. But the package was lost or misdirected. "We don't know what happened," said Helen. "Mr. Bryan offered to pay for them, but Mother didn't accept it because she hoped they would be found." Much to Bessie's disappointment, they never turned up.[11]

Bessie also took great pride in her flower beds, and an informal arrangement of garden flowers usually brightened the Marshall dinner table. Even when she was dressed for church, she could seldom resist the urge to stop by a flower bed and pull out a few weeds. Her Halifax garden featured masses of petunias lining a horseshoe-shaped drive, which were once photographed for a seed catalogue. At her final home in Portsmouth, she maintained a colorful garden, which "the mailman said had the nicest flowers of anyone's on the route," Helen noted.[12]

The WPA Commission

When Bessie Marshall began to paint more seriously, it was primarily to earn money for her family. The Marshalls moved to Petersburg in January 1937. Parkinson's disease had begun taking a toll on Myron's health; he was having trouble walking and enunciating and was losing his sight. Before retiring altogether, he accepted a two-month assignment at St. Paul's Church, a historic Gothic Revival structure where Robert E. Lee had worshiped during the siege of Petersburg. While the vestry looked for a permanent minister, the Marshalls lived in the rectory.

Across Union Street from the rectory lived Donald Holden, with whom Bessie soon developed a neighborly relationship. It was not long before Donald realized Bessie's talent, and it may have been Donald who arranged an exhibit of twenty-five of Bessie's floral paintings at a meeting of the Petersburg Garden Club on March 13, 1937.[13]

When the permanent minister arrived at St. Paul's at the end of March, the Marshalls looked for a rental house that the family could afford on Myron's pension. The house they found on St. Andrew Street —a one-story frame structure built in 1875, with tall windows and a wraparound porch—was something of a letdown to the teenaged Helen. "In Halifax we lived in a big house, and the rectory on Union Street was big," she said, "then I looked up on the hill and saw this little house."[14] But it was larger than it looked; it had seven rooms, including three bedrooms and a screened-in porch where some of the boys slept on bunk beds. The house had a big, gently sloping yard with shade trees and room for flower beds, and was situated in a pleasant neighborhood, within strolling distance of the local bandstand. Lieutenant Run, the stream into which the waters of Willcox Lake flowed, ran behind the Marshall house, forming a literal link to Lee Park, which would figure so prominently in Bessie's Petersburg life.

Although the Marshalls were careful not to discuss money with the children, finances were becoming a real concern. Myron's pension

Bessie Marshall in 1937, the year she began painting the Lee Park wildflowers. (Courtesy of Helen Marshall Fedziuk.)

could not cover the rent and bills, and debts to the grocer began to mount. In addition, two grandchildren—Bobby and Anne Hoffman, Louise's son and daughter—lived with Myron and Bessie much of the time. Some of the older children had jobs and helped out, but Bessie still felt the need for an additional source of income. The commission to paint the wildflowers in the Lee Park WPA sanctuary came at just the right time, and Bessie readily accepted.

It was an ideal pairing of subject and artist. Bessie had a deep affection for wildflowers. "They are like fairies," she once said in a newspaper interview, explaining her attraction. "You come upon one in the woods one day and you go back later to paint it and it has vanished."[15]

In March 1937, Bessie began painting the Lee Park wildflowers. She kept a small logbook containing a partial record of the dates and hours worked and the paintings completed. The earliest date given is March 9, 1937, for her painting of trailing arbutus. Other works from spring 1937 include her flowering dogwood, five-finger, and blue lupine.[16]

Bessie painted from live specimens that came from the Lee Park sanctuary and surrounding areas, and she attained a high level of skill in a relatively short time. Sometimes Donald Holden, who owned a car, brought the specimens to her; other times Donald would drive Bessie to Lee Park, where she would collect flowers herself.[17] Bessie's logbook suggests she did not necessarily paint from the same specimens that Donald pressed. According to the labels on the specimens of the herbarium collection, the plants that were pressed and dried were sometimes collected days or even weeks earlier (and in a few cases, later) than the logbook dates for the corresponding paintings.[18]

Bessie liked to paint outside in the afternoons, usually on the porch, but sometimes at a table in the side yard near the swing set. She would hold up her specimen to the afternoon light, studying the plant's subtle points and examining it from different angles. Occasionally, she painted indoors, on a card table near the bay window of the living room. She also did some painting on site at Lee Park.

Often Bessie worked five or six hours each day, and some days up to ten hours. She painted through the seasons, from the prairie willow of late winter to the field-thistle of mid-autumn. According to her logbook, she spent at least 809 hours painting the Lee Park watercolors in 1938, 762 hours in 1939, and 103 hours in 1940, for a total of at least 1,674 hours. In some instances, the log indicates how many hours she spent painting a particular plant, which ranged from two hours for snakeroot to ten hours for lizard's tail and rosin-weed. Because the log is incomplete, these figures may be on the low side.[19]

How much Bessie was paid for her wildflower paintings, and from which precise sources, is not entirely clear; no paycheck stubs or other

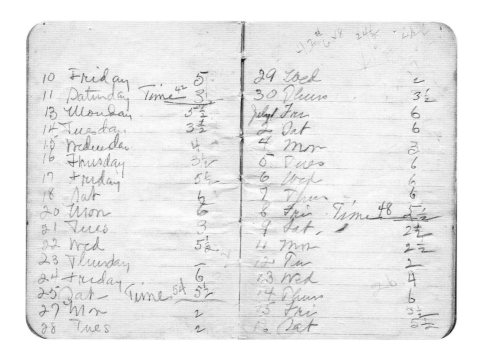

A page from Bessie Marshall's logbook, in which she kept track of the hours she spent painting the Lee Park watercolors. (Courtesy of Helen Marshall Fedziuk.)

records have been found. Her family remembers her being paid mostly from WPA funds (although apparently not through the Federal Art Project). The Petersburg Garden Club also contributed some funding, but when and how much is not known. A final group of paintings, commissioned in 1947, was paid for entirely with garden club funds. A notebook of Donald Holden's refers to a twenty-dollar appropriation made by the garden club during that time for four wildflower paintings, to "complete the Herbarium of Lee Park Wildflowers—the paintings to be done by the same artist."[20] Bessie apparently finished these four paintings—the Carolina-lily, chinquapin, hoary mountain-mint, and joe-pye weed—in early 1948, before the herbarium collection won the Massie Medal.

Technique and Style

Bessie bought her supplies from a stationery store on Sycamore Street in downtown Petersburg.[21] She used watercolors in tubes and painted on medium-weight, off-white rag paper with a smooth surface that gave a crisp quality to minute details. It was also a somewhat unforgiving paper that demanded skill in applying the watercolor, but Bessie had a steady hand.[22] Rather than transferring a sketch from a separate page, she apparently sketched directly onto the paper in very light pencil. (Very few of her watercolors have obvious pencil marks, but a sketch of a twig can be seen at the bottom of her illustration of the strawberry bush on page 164.)

To represent the subtle colors of flowers like bluets, Bessie used a light wash; for plants with more brilliant color, like the day-lily, she built up intensity with layers of wash. Sometimes, as in the white-topped aster, she allowed the color of the background paper to represent the ivory of the ray florets. But in plants with densely clustered florets or snow-white flowers, she used gouache to achieve effects that would be extremely difficult to produce using watercolor alone. She also used gouache to capture certain opaque textures, such as the fuzzy leaves of the mullein. In one of her two paintings of partridge-berry, she experimented with an eighteenth-century convention of using a black background to dramatize the bright red of the berries.

Botanical illustration demands foremost that its practitioners reproduce a plant with accuracy and attention to characteristics that will help people identify it. Bessie excelled at rendering the details of plant morphology—nodes, veins, flowers, pubescence (hairiness) on leaves and stems, and glaucousness (whitish film) on berries and leaves. Some of her paintings contain near-microscopic details, such as the halo of anthers surrounding a catkin of prairie willow or the small yellow spots on a petal of pickerel-weed. Sometimes she painted certain details more crisply to pull them toward the foreground, as in her rendering of the five hoods and five horns of the white milkweed flower. To achieve this level of detail, Bessie used a brush so tiny it seemed like a wondrous invention to her daughter Bits.[23] In her most polished works— the hazel-nut, for example—she had the brush control needed to paint such sharp details as the double-toothed leaf and the speckled catkins, while keeping a loose enough hand to convey the ruffles of the nut husk.

Bessie generally took a traditional approach to botanical illustration. Many of her paintings are close to life-size. For plants too tall to fit on standard-size paper, like the colic-root, she alluded to their height by painting sections of the stem alongside each other. (And some paintings were trimmed to fit into the herbarium collection albums.) Sometimes she included fruits, bulbs, and roots along with flowers and leaves, or depicted a plant in subsequent stages of bud, bloom, and fruit (as she did with the parachuted fruits of the leopard's-bane).

Yet within this essentially conservative medium, she found room for personal expression. In her jack-in-the-pulpit, for example, she unified a complex composition by echoing the curves of the "pulpits" in the arc of a withered stem. Occasionally she gave her paintings an earthy charm by including a plant's imperfections, such as the blemished leaf in her mountain laurel.

Bessie had an intuitive sense of composition. In some of her water-colors, like the spring-beauty, she used the bulb and roots to contrast with the wispy fragility of the stems and flowers. For others, like the wild potato-vine, she accentuated the plant's graceful lines by leaving ample white space in the background. Rather than depicting a plant head-on, she often chose to highlight two different views of a flower or to show both the top and the underside of the leaves. Her Carolina-lily, for example, shows the flowers from three different angles.

Bessie had a strong feel for the individual nature of each plant, from the animated pinwheels of the periwinkle flower to the blocky skunk-cabbage. Her patient rendering of the pokeweed, for example, empha-sizes the lush berries of what some might consider a homely garden weed. "She really loved the flowers and saw different expressions in each one," wrote Louise Marshall McCrensky, her eldest child.[24]

These accomplishments are especially remarkable when one con-siders that Bessie's home life was not always conducive to serious, sustained work. Some of the older children had moved away, but they often came back to visit, and the younger children led typically active teenage lives. Myron's condition was growing worse; he was virtually blind, and he needed Bessie's help to eat and do other routine tasks. But his mind was still very much intact, which made him frustrated and anxious. Listening to the radio and hearing Bessie read letters from the children were among his few pleasures. "I think Papa depends so much on hearing from you all, as he has nothing in the world, and he feels things much more than ever," Bessie wrote to her daughter Catherine in 1938.[25]

In October 1938, Donald Holden organized a display of Bessie's wildflower paintings for the WPA booth at the Petersburg fair. "They were very much admired," Donald wrote, "and they were so natural looking that one visitor thought they were real flowers." By the end of 1939, Bessie had completed approximately two hundred paintings. Her output tapered off after that. Myron required greater care, and her own health had begun to suffer from the stress. In April 1940, Bessie wrote: "I have been too busy with my outside and home work and today in the woods suddenly I couldn't see but the right half of everything —but after a dose of ammonia & lying down a spell I got O.K."[26] Some of her finer works, such as lizard's tail and day-lily, were done in 1940. The last date mentioned in her logbook was August 9, 1940, for the black huckleberry, although it is possible some of the undated entries may have been done later that year. In any case, the WPA project was ending, and Bessie focused her energies on finding other commissions. She did not resume painting the Lee Park wildflowers until 1947 or 1948.

Seeking Wider Recognition

Painting the Lee Park wildflowers boosted Bessie Marshall's confidence, and she began to think of herself as a professional artist. Although some Petersburg families had commissioned her to do oil paintings of botanical subjects, her real hope was to establish a reputation beyond the local area and earn more money. In the late 1930s, she began sending out letters and samples of her work to publishing companies, magazines, and other outlets that might reproduce her paintings or commission her as an illustrator.

In the fall of 1938, after seeing excerpts from a book by another botanical painter in the *National Geographic,* Bessie decided to submit her own paintings to the publisher. In a letter to her daughter Catherine, she described what happened during a trip to Washington, D.C.

[W]ith designs in my heart I took my pictures. It was my ambition to get an audience with the "head man" at the National Geographic. Well, the long and short of it—I did, and he took his book of flowers that they describe in the foreword as having been painted by the "world's greatest living wildflower painter" and tried to see what she had that I haven't got. Mr. Edwards of the Nat. Geog. said he acknowledged that mine were better . . . but he would not pass on them from a botanical standpoint, so he sent me to Mr. Morrison who is head of the botany department at the Bureau of Agriculture for his opinion

—and it was most flattering. I told him I would like to have myself called the "world's best living wildflower painter" & he told me I need take a title from no one but could create my own.[27]

Edwards told Bessie that the *National Geographic* planned to compile a volume of the flowers of the eastern region within a year or two and asked her whether she would be able to travel the eastern seaboard. "I have not been asked to sign on any dotted line," she wrote, "but I am all puffed up with having had a lovely visit." Nothing ultimately came out of the meeting, however. Moreover, Bessie's obligations at home made it difficult for her to travel, even to Richmond. "I was going to . . . go to Richmond to an Artists' Evening, where I was asked to exhibit some pictures," she wrote in 1939, "but Pa was feeling so bad all day I phoned I couldn't go."[28]

In 1939 Bessie tried to interest the Macmillan Company in publishing a book of her wildflower paintings. Although the director of the outdoor book division complimented her "splendid" paintings, this contact did not bear fruit, either. As Bessie explained to Helen in a letter of October 5, "They are still interested but say 'due to world conditions they are afraid to bring out my book now.' It would cost about $75,000 to do what I want and they don't think it wise to break up the idea. They have me on their files as a special illustrator. . . . But I haven't much hope."[29]

Bessie sent her botanical illustrations to *Life* magazine in 1940, but to no avail. Meanwhile, she gained admirers at two universities. Dr. E. C. L. Miller of the Medical College of Virginia in Richmond declared that her paintings were "the real thing" and offered to display them at the college library; it is not known whether he did. H. L. Blomquist of the Department of Botany at Duke University gave Bessie encouragement in a 1941 letter: "You are doing excellent work. . . . I wish I was so situated that I could employ you, but that will have to wait."[30]

Bessie's attitude about these setbacks wavered between dejection and hopefulness. In 1940 she wrote to Helen, "I started so late to get my million, I'm afraid I will stop a little short—but maybe not," adding that "I've got a motto; 'always merry and glad.'"[31]

In the early 1940s, Bessie tried marketing hand-painted trays through interior decorators and *House and Garden* magazine. "At present I'm tray-minded," she wrote Helen; "not a form of insanity but I am painting trays. I did the one that caught the water under the dish drainer and it's *rale* pretty—also a large old one for L. Annie (for some money Pa owed her) and am doing the one that graced our fireplace." An advertisement in the September 1941 issue of *House and Garden* included a picture of a hand-painted floral tray with this enticement: "Flowers as lovely as any that grow in your garden, painted especially for you on any size or shape tray. Each flower, each leaf is botanically correct; the colors exquisite." Readers were invited to contact the artist, Mrs. B. N. Marshall. This national exposure brought sales from as far away as California, and nibbles from elsewhere, but Bessie could not sell enough trays to afford to keep an inventory on hand. "Evidently my prices [ten dollars a tray] don't appeal to the majority," she wrote Helen.[32]

A promising opportunity arose in 1944, when the *Encyclopedia Britannica* was looking for artists to draw wildflowers for its junior edition. Bessie had been recommended by a contact at *National Geographic*. A series of meetings and communications ensued, with Bessie growing anxious as she waited for each response. Finally, after learning that Bessie's situation prevented her from doing much traveling, a *Britannica* editor asked her to draw two examples of wildflowers from her local area, "which will be my 'entrance exam,'" she wrote to her son Pinky. "I want to do this more than I have ever wanted to do anything (except the war to be over) for myself & at my age probably the opportunity won't knock again," she wrote. "If I succeed at this it may lead to bigger & better but if I can't do this—exit."[33]

Bessie sent off illustrations of trillium and azalea, for which she was paid sixty dollars. She wrote to Helen in March 1945: "Ency. Brit. likes my pictures. . . . It takes me two days (plus or minus) to do one but altogether not a bad day's work—for I do many thises and thats besides the picture." The *Britannica* editors liked her sample paintings well enough to continue to the proof stage. But then, as Louise recalled, "the blow fell." *Britannica* was sold to another company, which decided it would be more cost-effective to photograph the flowers instead of commissioning drawings. "It was a great disappointment that it didn't come to pass," said Helen.[34]

Bessie also approached the National Wildlife Federation in late 1944 about doing wildflower art for postage stamps. "I sent them some real pretty ones I borrowed from the Library so expected a telegram or a delegation to visit me," she told Helen in a letter. "Well—time will tell. . . . Maybe anticipation is a greater pleasure than the reality will be." The federation officials commended her work, but none of her paintings met their strict specifications for color, size, borders, and paper. They suggested she do a design for a goldenrod stamp that did meet their criteria, but she could not find the right paper in Petersburg and abandoned the effort.[35]

By the mid-1940s, Bessie had achieved some popularity as a garden club speaker. In a letter to Helen, she described a 1944 speech with characteristic diffidence: "Not having a corner to which to flee—as long as it is only about what I've done or some such I couldn't refuse."

By 1945, Myron was suffering from the later stages of Parkinson's disease, and Bessie could seldom find the time to paint. "[Encyclopedia Britannica] wants an azalea," she wrote to Helen. "I had two so [I] sent them both for them to take their pick just to stall for time, for I cannot have a minute's leisure when there's nobody to help me here. It took me four hours just to write a letter to one of them."[36]

One of her last serious attempts to market her work took place in the late 1940s, when her son Pinky, then a student at the University of Virginia, was working part-time for Paul Victorius, a Charlottesville art dealer with a framing business. Victorius entertained the idea of publishing prints of several rose paintings that Bessie had done, but after testing a few he decided it was too costly to reproduce them. He did produce a print of her painting of assorted garden flowers, which remains in the family. Pinky also showed a few of his mother's wildflower paintings to Colgate Darden, then president of the University of Virginia. Darden wrote Bessie: "They are perfectly beautiful and I should like so to acquire a set of them for the Library here at the University. Work of that excellence should be preserved in the archives of the State University."[37] But no commission ever followed, and Bessie turned her attention to matters at home.

Later Life

The year 1946 was a difficult one for Bessie. Myron died in Petersburg on January 9. Then in March, her fifteen-year-old grandson Bobby, who was still living with her, came home from the movies one night complaining of a headache. Bessie was in the hospital at the time for a minor operation, and Bobby's mother, Louise, was staying at Bessie's house. Bobby very quickly fell ill, and the next evening, March 30, he died of what the doctors believed was spinal meningitis. His death was a major blow to the already distressed family. "Mother was ignored in the hospital while we were cleansing the house with antiseptics as we were advised to do by the health department," said Helen. "It makes me very sad to think of her intense grieving alone."[38]

After these two losses, Bessie decided to return to Portsmouth, where many relatives and friends from her youth still lived. Her son Richard built her a house at Swimming Point, just a few blocks from where she grew up. Here she resumed an active life, joining a literary society, playing bridge, becoming involved with her church, and planting flowers. She did some paintings of family coats of arms, Confederate flags, and flowers. She spoke at garden clubs throughout the state, often illustrating her talks with her paintings.

Bessie took considerable joy in her grandchildren. According to her grandson Bruce Marshall, she was a generous grandmother "with a Mother Goose sort of smile and warmth," as well as "a remarkable ability to make me feel like I was the most delightful child in the world." Her grandchildren especially liked the trinkets she gave them—a foreign coin and a miniature Greyhound bus were two that Bruce remembered. Decades later he still treasured his moonstone collection, which Bessie "selected only after picking up and examining numerous little stones—looking at each for color and shape—and then she gave them all to me, only one of her thirty-some grandchildren."[39]

Bessie Marshall died of a stroke at age seventy-five, on Valentine's Day of 1960. Her niece Betsy MacKenzie, who was living next door at the time, recalled the circumstances: "We had a little bell that went from her bed past the window [to our house] for her to ring if she needed us. . . . It rang just twice. That night she died."[40] Just the day before, Bessie had gone outside in the snow to check on her rose bush.

Years later, her daughters would sometimes think about their mother's life—her devotion to her family and the limited recognition she received for her art—and they would wonder whether she had been happy. "Most of mother's life she thought wonderful things were going to happen, but they never quite came through," said Bits. But, Helen added, "We believe she did have a happy life."[41]

Bessie Marshall's surviving relatives own some of her work. Her grandson Richard Marshall inherited both a painting of a rose and one of her sketch pads. "The roses are beautiful, but the ones on the pad are very interesting," he said. "There's a thumbprint on one, where she had paint on her finger, and you can see where the paint has been spilled." Bessie's family still remembers her optimistic outlook. As her niece Katharine wrote, "In the ups and downs of my own long life, I have said out loud to myself, 'How would Bessie handle this?'"[42]

THREE

The WPA Wildflower and Bird Sanctuary

A Garden of Women's Work

"We worked through Dec. cleaning up the woods and the ravines. . . . We made compost heaps with some of the leaves to use on our flowers . . . [and] covered the bare spots with leaves. We cleared the ten acres we are using for our project of the decayed limbs and old flower stalks, scattering the seeds as we gathered them."[1]

This was how Mary Webb Jones described her first weeks of work in 1935 as a forewoman on the Lee Park Wildflower and Bird Sanctuary in Petersburg. Mary and her all-female crew were responsible for clearing and planting one of the sanctuary's four hills. "Mrs. Jones's Hill" descended through a forest of northern red oak, chestnut oak, and tulip-tree, across marshy ground where cat-tails found a receptive habitat, and down to the edge of Willcox Lake.

By the following spring, the workers had made substantial progress. On the hillsides they planted blue-eyed grass, wild ginger, wild columbine, bloodroot, mountain laurel, and a profusion of other wildflowers and shrubs. In the lowlands they planted red chokeberry, spotted touch-me-not, lizard's tail, jack-in-the-pulpit, and a few dozen other species. "[T]he public is invited at the present time to visit the wild flower preserve in Lee Park to see the violets and azaleas now in bloom," read a notice in the local newspaper in April 1936. By August the women had created a full-fledged nature preserve, with paths, benches, and

The workers and supervisors of the WPA Wildflower and Bird Sanctuary in Lee Park, March 1936. This area—the heart of the sanctuary—was located just above a major inlet of Willcox Lake where a system of ravines fed into the WPA "bog." (Courtesy of Tim Richard.)

markers. An article in the local newspaper described its attractions: "Visitors to the flower sanctuary follow trails, marked off by pine brush, which lead through four valleys and their surrounding areas. No less than 354 kinds of flowers are to be seen, all of them marked with their ordinary and their botanical names in such a manner that anyone can inform himself in this respect. Many flowers are in bloom at this time, although the coming of fall is expected to make the sanctuary even more beautiful."[2]

For Mary Webb Jones, a WPA job offered more than an opportunity to beautify a city park; it meant she could support herself and her daughter. Mary's husband milled and sold lumber in Smithfield,

Virginia, but with the onset of the Great Depression, people stopped buying, daughter Marian Jones Baughman recalled. The family pinned its hopes on the oldest son, Winston, a college student who seemed destined for a good job. But Winston died in a car accident in 1931, and his death devastated the family. Mary suffered an emotional collapse. She and her husband separated, and as soon as she was well enough, she moved herself and Marian to Petersburg, where they shared an apartment above a shoe store with a cousin's family. The death of her son and the separation from her husband "took away what my mother thought was going to be," Marian explained. "She realized she had to do it herself." In 1934, Mary found work as a practical nurse in a health project funded by the Federal Emergency Relief Administration. In 1935, she transferred to a supervisory job with the WPA sanctuary project, where she could apply the skills she had learned growing up on a farm.[3]

On the west end of Petersburg, Lillian Anderson, a mother of seven children (later eleven), realized "she had to do something to help raise us," said her daughter Percilla Anderson. Lillian's husband had gone to Baltimore to find work. "Times were hard—I didn't realize how hard until I got older," Percilla recalled. Finally a WPA job came through. According to her daughter Marion Anderson, Lillian could handle any kind of tool and had learned a lot about plants from her mother, who was an American Indian—skills that came in handy in Lee Park.[4]

These two women's situations were not unlike those of the scores of women who held WPA jobs at one time or another in the Lee Park sanctuary. For many women, including project supervisor Donald Holden, the WPA itself represented a kind of sanctuary. "Down through the ages whenever and wherever there has arisen a great need, a sanctuary has been provided," Donald wrote in 1938, in an unpublished paper about the project. "The Works Progress Administration of America is a sanctuary for all who work under her red, white, and blue emblem."[5]

Getting Started

In November 1935, the city of Petersburg applied to the WPA to sponsor a wildflower sanctuary project with a proposed cost of $45,000. The sanctuary project had multiple goals: to create jobs, to preserve native flora and fauna, to beautify a community park, and to develop an "outdoor classroom" where schoolchildren and others could learn about the habits of plants and birds. The project was approved, with the city as the main local sponsor, and the first federal allocation of $11,425 came through in early December 1935. Over the next five years, more than $127,000 would be spent on the project, with the city of Petersburg contributing from 6 to 27 percent of the costs at various points of the project.[6]

Community organizations also pitched in. The focus on preserving native plants held a natural appeal for the Petersburg Garden Club and fit nicely with the conservation mission of the Garden Club of Virginia. The Petersburg Garden Club agreed to cosponsor the sanctuary, providing technical assistance, funding, publicity, and local advocacy. "When I needed advice, help, and courage, I found it in Garden Club members," wrote Donald Holden in her notes for a 1948 presentation. Garden club members joined with a host of other civic organizations to encourage people to purchase dogwood and redbud trees at a cost of a dollar each. Some five hundred trees were planted in the sanctuary as "living memorials to friends, relatives, members, or distinguished citizens." The Chamber of Commerce endorsed the sanctuary project, and local businesses donated equipment and materials. The General Garment Manufacturers furnished seventy-five pounds of fabric scraps for bird nesting materials, and the Norfolk and Western Railroad, whose tracks bordered Lee Park, contributed lumber to build shelters.[7]

For the site of the sanctuary, the city initially set aside ten wooded acres on the west side of Lee Park, a section that included a variety of habitats. Later the preserve was expanded to twenty-five acres.

Meanwhile, New Deal programs were subsidizing other construction and service projects in and around the park. Men employed through the Civil Works Administration, a predecessor to the WPA, cleared brush, thinned out damaged trees, constructed guardrails and footpaths, graded a baseball diamond, and expanded the shallow swimming area of the lake. Funds from the Federal Emergency Relief Administration were used to build a new bathhouse and replace the rotting diving tower. A WPA-funded subsistence garden in the northwest section of the park provided food for the city's hungry. Men from a Civilian Conservation Corps camp at the Petersburg National Battlefield Park did planting and erosion control around the Civil War breastworks (which had been under the care of the National Park Service since 1927).[8]

To oversee the sanctuary project, the city hired Donald Holden as a noncertified WPA employee. (Noncertified workers included supervisory personnel who did not come from the relief rolls, but who had relevant experience.) Donald's horticultural knowledge and supervisory experience in the WPA subsistence garden made her well-suited to the task. A capable administrator with a great deal of energy, Donald had a dignified presence that belied a friendly personality, a fondness for wordplay, and a self-deprecating humor that emerged in her personal correspondence. Donald also had a strong work ethic: "Remember to always do more than is expected of you and you'll get ahead," she advised her son in a 1940 letter.[9]

Donald Claiborne Holden

Mary Donald Fraser Claiborne was born in Petersburg on November 10, 1890, to John Herbert Claiborne and Annie Leslie Watson Claiborne. John Herbert was a medical doctor who had set up practice in Petersburg as a young man and had served terms in both the Virginia House of Delegates and the state senate. During the Civil War, Dr. Claiborne became senior surgeon in charge of the Petersburg military hospitals, where he tended legions of wounded. A learned man, he was, by his own description, "fond of quiet," and he valued education, propriety, and civic duty. "If [a man] left no fortune at his death," he wrote in his memoirs published in 1904, "he left the inheritance of a good name crowned with the memory of good deeds, done unselfishly and in secret."[10]

Donald's mother, Annie Watson, was the daughter of a Scottish businessman who had settled in Petersburg. Some forty years younger than John Herbert, Annie was the doctor's second wife (his first had died in 1869). According to a family story, young Annie, who had grown up across the street from the Claibornes, was originally courted by John Herbert's grown son from his first marriage. When the son was called away on business, he told his father to look after Annie while he was gone. Not only did Dr. Claiborne look after her, he eventually married her. In addition to Donald, the couple had a son, Robert Claiborne, who in later life raised tropical flowers in the Virgin Islands and Puerto Rico. Annie made her own reputation in the community as one of the founders of the Petersburg Home for Ladies, a residence for elderly women. Donald and her mother were very close. "Her mother was more like her older sister," Donald's son Herbert Holden recalled.[11]

When Donald was seventeen, her father died. She graduated from Petersburg High School, then completed her education at Southern Female College, a local institution. On June 10, 1915, she married Stephen West Holden, an officer of a trunk- and bag-manufacturing business that had been in the Holden family until another company bought it out. A "large and fashionable assemblage" attended the Claiborne-Holden wedding, according to a newspaper announcement, and Donald's fondness for flowers was much in evidence. The Tabb Street Presbyterian church was decorated with palms, ferns, and southern smilax, and the Claiborne home at 109 North Union Street was adorned with pink roses and sweet peas. One of the songs played during the ceremony was "To a Wild Flower."[12]

Donald Claiborne Holden and her family, Christmas 1943. Left to right: Annie Watson (Nan), Donald Claiborne (daughter), John, Annie Watson (daughter) holding her baby Robert McKean, Herbert, and Donald. Donald sent this photograph to her son West, who was in the Navy at the time. (Courtesy of Herbert Holden.)

During their early years of marriage, Donald and West Holden lived on Perry Street in Petersburg. In a span of just two and a half years, she gave birth to two girls and a boy: Annie Watson, Donald Claiborne, and Stephen West Holden. Two other children followed: Herbert Randall and John Gregory.

In 1925, the family moved to a house on Berkeley Avenue, where they lived for the next eight years. Here Donald perfected her gardening skills, subscribing to gardening magazines and sending away for seed catalogues. She designed a geometrical garden, seventy-five feet square, with four walkways radiating diagonally from a central hub. In her Haldean Gardens, as she called them, Donald planted iris, lily of the valley, handsome boxwoods, and other flowers and shrubs. Her gardens yielded many prize-winning flowers, and Donald often participated in garden shows as a competitor or judge. "I'm going down to the flower show to classify the iris," she wrote to Herbert in 1941.

"Do you remember when you and Daddy would always come and help me bring them home, and Daddy was always so proud of the blue ribbons I received."[13]

The family's circumstances took an abrupt, sad turn the summer of 1933, when West Holden was stricken with a form of meningitis. Three weeks later he died at age forty-eight. It was the middle of the Great Depression in Virginia, and the trunk and bag industry had bottomed out. Donald was left with her five children, now aged eight through sixteen, and with a mound of debts. She was a deeply religious woman—a friend of the Holden children remembered Donald leading them in prayer before they went out to play—and her faith apparently helped to carry her through the trauma of her husband's death. "Sometimes God lets a stinging blow fall upon our life," she counseled Herbert in a letter some years later. "The soul cries out in agony. The blow seems to you an awful mistake, but it is not, for you are the most priceless jewel in the world to God. Not a blow will be permitted to fall upon your shrinking soul, but that the love of God permits it."[14]

Donald struggled along, cutting corners wherever she could—she even took a leave of absence from the garden club—and the children helped out, too. She gave up her house, and she and the children moved in with her mother on Union Street. According to a family story, Donald was sitting on the porch one day, not long after she had moved in, when a neighbor stopped by to ask how she was doing. Donald replied, "We'll get along, I reckon; the Lord will look after me." Just then her mother poked her head out the door and said, "Yes, and I'm the Lord."[15] The family coped, and Donald seemingly appreciated her mother's help and companionship. Annie Claiborne took care of many household duties, while Donald started looking for a job.

Although Donald had not worked outside the home during her married life, she had a solid education and good leadership and organizational skills. She also had a head for figures; she avidly read the financial pages, and as soon as she started earning money, she invested small sums in the stock market.[16]

Donald was hired to oversee the WPA subsistence garden, and this in turn led to the Lee Park sanctuary job. She threw herself whole-heartedly into her work, which turned out to be both demanding and rewarding. Her dedication did not go unrecognized. "Mrs. Holden, a housewife who turned [landscape] engineer and converted her love of flowers and birds to a profitable profession, has received high commendation of her supervisors for the proficiency of her landscaping of the project," said a 1936 article in the *Petersburg Progress-Index*.[17]

The Workers

Putting unemployed people to work was the main goal of the sanctuary project. During its five years of federal funding, the sanctuary employed probably hundreds of women, often for short periods of time. Very few of their names are known.[18] As with most WPA projects, there was a fair amount of turnover in Lee Park. WPA jobs were meant to be temporary, to tide people over until they found work in the private sector. It was not unusual for someone to work on a WPA project for a month or two, then leave when a job opened up in the factories or in seasonal occupations. Some people were transferred from one WPA project to another, and others were let go because of supervisor dissatisfaction. The number of job slots on a particular project also rose and fell with changes in federal allocations.

In addition to Donald Holden, who rotated between the park and the local WPA office, the typical workforce at the sanctuary included a timekeeper, four to eight supervisors (called forewomen), and several dozen laborers. The number of employees fluctuated, depending on how much federal money was available and how much work needed to be done. Between June 1937 and June 1938, the average workforce on the project ranged from 61 to 99; between June 1938 and October 1938, after an erosion control component had been added, the number of employees ranged from 102 to 128. Nearly all of them were women, although a few men were hired to cut steps; help construct bridges, benches, and shelters; and do other heavy work.[19]

All available evidence indicates that the work roles in the sanctuary were segregated; the laborers were black and the forewomen were white, mirroring institutionalized patterns in employment, education, and other social enterprises in the South during the 1930s. The black and white employees reported to separate community centers for indoor work, and the forewomen apparently had access to some perquisites that the laborers did not, such as a brick warming fireplace and a sheltered lunchroom.[20] This type of segregation was typical of many New Deal projects in the South. Although federal WPA regulations prohibited racial discrimination, there were discrepancies in many communities between the stated policies and actual practices, and the Roosevelt administration chose not to push the point too vigorously because President Roosevelt did not want to lose political support for his New Deal in the southern states so vital to his reelection. Throughout the South, sewing rooms, Civilian Conservation Corps camps, and other New Deal programs operated in segregated facilities, and educated blacks seldom received assignments appropriate to their talents and training. These situations gave rise to criticisms about discrimination. Advocacy groups documented cases in several states where black workers were assigned to do more onerous work than whites at lower rates of pay or were mistreated on the job. At the same time, black leaders and black voters recognized the WPA's crucial role in providing financial support to black families, and they generally supported the program despite its flaws.[21]

Under WPA guidelines, 90 percent of the employees had to come from the rolls of needy heads of households who had applied for relief. Many Petersburg women who sought WPA jobs were in dire straits. "I buy beans, peas, herring [and] white meat, trying to stretch. The children have no nourishing [food] as they should," said Catherine Johnson, a former Lee Park worker, in a 1939 oral-history interview with WPA writer Susie Byrd.[22] Some of the WPA workers lived in dilapidated houses in bottomland neighborhoods that were breeding grounds for typhoid and malaria. In the home of Minnie Price, another former

Lee Park worker, Byrd observed that "all the plastering is down in the room upstairs, and in the dormer window on the front, six window panes are out. Cold just sweeps through the house." Minnie told Byrd, "Next week I don't know where food and wood will come from."[23]

WPA wages had to be consistent with prevailing rates for similar work in a local community, but not so high as to discourage people from seeking private jobs. As a forewoman at Lee Park, Mary Webb Jones was paid $47.30 per month, while Anna E. Ross, who worked as a laborer, was paid $37.50 per month, according to her daughter Carrie McNear. Transportation was not provided, and getting to Lee Park presented a major obstacle for some. Lee Park worker Allie Jones "left home at 5 o'clock every morning to get to work by 7:30. The walk one way is, I guess, about 3 ½ miles." She observed that "walking so far took part of our strength before starting work for the day."[24]

Work Life in the Sanctuary

The typical workday began early in the morning and lasted eight hours, with some overtime to make up for rainy days. Worker Mary Bell Focie remembered her crew starting each day with a prayer. The workers were divided into crews, consisting of a forewoman and seven or eight laborers, and each crew was assigned to one of four hills, named for their outstanding features: Moss Hill, Glendale, Lakeside, and Fern Grotto. As the acreage expanded, crews fanned out into other sections of the park.

The women wore their own clothes—generally a long skirt or dress and a cloth coat in colder weather—and some wore galoshes provided by the federal government. Their tools included grubbing hoes that looked like short pickaxes, shovels, rakes, and spades. Most of the time they worked outdoors, but when the weather was very inclement, they moved indoors, where they received work-related training, wove baskets for collecting plants and other items, and made birdhouses, bags of suet, and nesting materials for the bird areas.[25]

For the first two years of the project, the bulk of the labor consisted of transplanting wildflowers, shrubs, and trees into the sanctuary. With the city's permission, the workers gathered plants from 1,500 acres[26] of municipal lands in and around Lee Park, then transplanted massive numbers of them into the preserve. "The workers make trips to the woods nearly every day and bring in shrubs and flowers," wrote Donald Holden in a project report. "Almost every flower and shrub common to Virginia has been brought in."[27] In a matter of months, the women had transplanted or planted 34,325 plants, representing more than 400 species; Donald Holden proudly noted that only 1,127 plants failed to thrive.[28]

Samuel Robinson, a nephew of Lillian Anderson's who sometimes went to the park to pick berries to sell, remembered seeing his aunt and her coworkers planting ferns on a washed-out section along the park road. "They would dig up the dirt and bank it up on the hills to shore up the road," he explained. "They had pans they put the dirt in. They put the pans on their heads—that was an old tradition, my grandmother could dance with a glass of water on her head—and they carried the pan up to the side of the hill and dropped it out."[29]

Creating bird habitats was another project activity. In a special area of the sanctuary, the workers erected rustic birdhouses and feeding stations. They sowed a strip of land with grain, planted evergreens that could shelter birds for the winter, and set out pan scratch, suet, and nesting materials. During one holiday season, a WPA monthly project report noted, they trimmed a "living Christmas tree" in the bird area, "decorated with ornaments, tinsel, strings of popcorn and cranberries, bread, and suet." A weekly census of birds confirmed the presence of up to one hundred different species at a given time. "The red-breasted nuthatch was seen for the first time recently," said the February 1939 monthly report. "Robins have returned in large numbers. The hermit thrush is very much in evidence. A few chickadees have been seen; they are believed to be migrating home. The juncos appear to be gathering for migration also."[30]

A bird shelter made of pine boughs in the Lee Park sanctuary, near a rustic bench (upper right) and a stand of wild cane (lower right). (Courtesy of Tim Richard.)

Other tasks were aimed at creating an inviting environment for visitors. The workers laid paths guiding visitors past wildflower groupings, bird feeding areas, and other points of interest. "I liked those little trails," recalled Ray Daniels, a Petersburg man who once worked as a guide in the sanctuary. "They were built on a nice grade so you could get down to the water." Alongside the plants and trees, the workers placed metal markers with botanical and common names. "I remember hundreds of those markers," said Herbert Holden. "[Mother] carried them in the car. They were painted green with a light spike." The women workers also laid bridges across streams, erected log stairways up steep hillsides, and set out rustic benches. Later on, they made entrance signs, while the male workers built an office, storage huts, and a shelter.[31]

In 1937, at the request of Petersburg city manager John Broome, the WPA project was expanded to include erosion control in a section of Lee Park that had been damaged by fire in 1934. To stop cascades of silt from clogging Lieutenant Run, a tributary of the Appomattox River, the women workers planted Japanese honeysuckle along roadsides and on the bare stream banks below the Willcox Lake dam. A local editorial alluded to "an improved method of planting" whereby honeysuckle roots were interwoven with broomsedge.[32]

Mary Bell Focie worked in this section of the park. "There was nothing there but dirt before. . . . We planted little shrubs on the hills, about [eight inches] tall," she explained. The honeysuckle planting was particularly strenuous, and sometimes it got very cold. For many years afterward, "I didn't want to hear the name Lee's Park," Mary Bell said, because it reminded her of "freezing with a shovel in our hands."[33]

According to both Mary Bell Focie and Samuel Robinson, two local black ministers complained to city officials about assigning black women to outdoor work while white women worked in sewing rooms. The laboriousness of the honeysuckle planting may have aggravated their concerns; moreover, some of the workers, including Lillian Anderson, were pregnant. "Reverend [L. C.] Johnson followed the head man around town," Samuel Robinson said. "I don't know who that man was, but if Reverend Johnson would see him on the street, he'd tell him it's not right to work these women like that." Eventually the city set up a sewing room for black women, Mary Bell said, to which she and some of the other Lee Park workers were reassigned.[34]

Percilla Anderson remembered her mother, Lillian, giving a somewhat different account, in which a white man of unknown name and position lodged a complaint with local officials. (Whether this happened at the same time as the events described by Mary Bell Focie is not clear.) "This white man used to sit up on the hill and watch the women work," Percilla said. "He'd talk to them as they left work and say, 'You all have no business doing that work, but something's going to be done about it.'" The man talked to the city officials, Percilla said, and after that, the women did less heavy digging and more flower planting.[35]

Two Lee Park workers interviewed by WPA writer Susie Byrd in 1939 also recounted some negative experiences on the job. Catherine Johnson described her experience in this way:

We had to carry large trees, two workers to a tree. . . . Some workers actually rolled gravel in wheelbarrows. . . . I had to dig and dig shrubbery and go up very steep hills. This made my breath short. (My weight is 200 lbs.) I just had to stop to rest between digs. It was for this reason the supervisor cut me off. She put on my slip "Careless Worker."

The day before I was cut off I sawed a cross cut saw: Martha Jane Buford at one end, and I at the other end. . . . It was very cold that day. The white workers sat by the fire all day, picking pine tags for making baskets and hats. We were not allowed to stop to warm until lunch time. This is the truth, no one knows but the one who goes through with it. We poor folks had to work this way or get nothing to do. We wanted to tell someone but didn't know where to go, because all the supervisors were white. . . . I want work & will work but I couldn't stand going to the park doing what I did last fall.[36]

Minnie Price, who worked on the honeysuckle planting project, also reported being laid off for similar reasons in her oral history: "Occasionally I would stop digging to catch my breath. When this supervisor saw me do this several times, she said I was a slacker and cut me off."[37]

Lillian Anderson did not experience these types of problems on the job, Percilla Anderson said, and her friendship with Mary Bell Focie and another neighbor who worked alongside her helped to pass the day. "I never heard my mother complain about anything the supervisors had done or said to her," Percilla said. "If they had, she would have straightened it out. She was an outspoken person." Percilla remembered her mother speaking of Donald Holden as a supervisor who had high expectations but was reasonable. Mary Bell, who did not remember Donald at all, said that some of the supervisors were amiable while others were contrary.[38]

The written documents about the project—which, of course, had a different purpose, origin, and intended audience than the oral histories—describe a congenial working environment and even some lighter moments.[39] These varying reports about what it was like to work in the sanctuary indicate, not surprisingly, that the black laborers faced more difficult circumstances than the white supervisors. They also suggest that, within either category, people perceived and dealt with similar situations in different ways. Samuel Robinson may have summed up the attitude of many workers when he described his Aunt Lillian's feelings about her WPA job. "They'd been so bad off, they were proud to get anything," he explained, "and if they got a job they were very happy just to have it."[40]

Preservation, Conservation, and Education

A main goal of the Lee Park sanctuary was to protect as many species of wildflowers as possible. As one way to accomplish this, species were transplanted into the sanctuary from other sections of the park and its environs, and some plants were brought in from up to eight miles away. "No plant is moved from its natural location unless we can provide an equally good one in the sanctuaries," Donald Holden explained.[41] Approaches to wildflower conservation have changed considerably since the 1930s. Preserving original habitats is far preferable to transplanting, and such practices as raking the grounds and planting en masse for visual effect have been repudiated. But the Lee Park sanctuary provides an interesting example of the thinking that prevailed at the time.[42]

Donald Holden was in touch with botanists in Richmond and elsewhere, and in developing the sanctuary she followed some of the advice of the Committee on Virginia Flora of the Virginia Academy of Science. She corresponded with Robert Smart, a member of the committee and curator of the University of Richmond herbarium. Smart offered her the use of his herbarium to help her identify plants found in Lee Park. Donald was probably the contributor of the specimen of pink milkwort in the University of Richmond herbarium, which was recorded as coming from Lee Park. This herbarium held several other specimens collected in or near Petersburg, including laurel-leaved greenbrier, Virginia wild ginger, ladies' tresses, orange milkwort, and a leopard's-bane specimen from Johnson Road, which borders Lee Park.[43]

News of the Lee Park sanctuary also reached botanist M. L. Fernald at Harvard University. In April 1939 he wrote to Donald: "[I] have looked with yearning eyes at the Lee Park Sanctuary and at the Military Park as I have driven through them. I hope that it will be possible to get a permit from you to look over the native flora in the Sanctuary, especially for the insignificant plants which are apt to be overlooked, but which may be of great botanical interest. When I next go to Petersburg, I will communicate with you, since both these areas contain so much unspoiled land that insignificant, but important, species may easily be lurking there as yet undetected."[44] Since Fernald does not mention Lee Park in his highly descriptive articles, he probably never made the trip.

The project supervisors kept records of the first bloom for every species and the length of time it lasted. Care was taken to transplant the rarer species into the more secluded recesses of the sanctuary. In a few instances, the project supervisors purchased plants not found in or near the park; this was the case for yellow lady's-slipper, skunk-cabbage, and pitcher-plant. Local citizens donated a few species, such as atamasco-lily and various irises. Altogether about 500 different species were transplanted or planted into the sanctuary.[45]

Then as now, it took vigilance to make sure that what was planted stayed planted. A 1936 newspaper notice urged the public "to refrain from picking wild flowers in Lee Park and especially in the wild flower preserve. Much time and labor has been devoted under a WPA project to preserving and arranging numerous specimens of wild flowers in the park, but in spite of this some individuals are continuing to remove plants from the park, either for their own gardens or from thoughtlessness."[46]

The project's conservation goals also extended to conservation of materials. Cleared limbs were reincarnated as wooden steps, bridges, and bird stations. Smaller branches and leaves fueled warming fires, and ashes from the fires in turn fertilized the plants. Tar drums from the city dump served as fireplaces, and discarded buckets became watering cans. Donald Holden brought in craftspeople, such as a local black basketmaker, to give the workers short courses on how to weave baskets out of oak splints, make wreaths out of evergreen branches, and craft hats, slippers, coasters, and flower potholders out of pine needles. ("Why buy a hat when they can be made of pine tags to have so much style and beauty?" remarked one woman upon seeing an exhibit of these articles.) At Christmas time, some of the workers sold their handicrafts for extra income. "The wreaths were sold at 75¢ and 35¢ each and the candle holders at 25¢ each," noted a monthly project report. "A table centerpiece of evergreens made by one of the workers was sold at $1.25."[47]

Educating people—both the workers and the public—about plants and birds was another major goal of the project. Ellen Woodward, the national head of the WPA Women's Division, stressed the need to provide women WPA workers with practical skills that would help them obtain private-sector jobs. In the sanctuary, this translated into training the workers for jobs as private gardeners, but it is not known how many actually found private jobs in related fields. The workers were taught planting and gardening techniques, plant identification, and other facts about flowers and birds. Donald Holden provided much of the instruction herself. To help the WPA employees remember plant names and other facts, Donald and the other supervisors told stories and Indian legends and devised games and contests. One game posed riddles whose answers were names of wildflowers. "A game and a small fruit" was the checkerberry, and "untamed sweetness" was the wild honeysuckle. Workers also made their own reference books about birds and flowers. Some of the supervisors became "so interested in their work they are ordering books on nature from a publishing house in New York and are sending to Washington for information on wild flowers and birds," a project report noted.[48]

The forewomen received additional training in botany, supervision, and first aid. The latter came in handy for Mary Webb Jones when a worker was bitten by a snake. "I, Mrs. Jones, gave first aid," she proudly reported. "Mrs. Holden took [the victim] in to a Dr. for treatment. The Dr. gave an excellent report as to the first aid rendered."[49]

More than anything, Donald hoped to create a "nature laboratory" where visitors could enjoy the outdoors and learn at the same time. To attract visitors and publicize the project, she sent information to newspapers, wrote articles for statewide magazines, gave radio talks, and mounted exhibits. At the 1937 Petersburg fair, the WPA sanctuary booth featured a "Wardian Case"—a glassed-in tabletop garden filled with partridge-berry, Indian pipe, ladies' tresses, and various mosses. The next year the exhibit included a box of honeysuckle "planted in a v-shape just as it is planted at Lee Park to prevent erosion," a report said.[50]

These efforts paid off, and visitors came from many states to admire the sanctuary and get ideas for other wildflower conservation projects. During one week in 1940, 373 people visited. After one busy season, Donald observed, "the city library says books on [birds and flowers] are in such demand they can't keep them on the shelves." Among those who paid visits were gardeners, horticulturists, and WPA officials from Virginia, Alabama, and Wisconsin. In June 1937, Ella Agnew came to Lee Park and brought along a Richmond colleague and a WPA publicity person from Washington, D.C.; according to a monthly report, "They were very much pleased with the work that is being done." During Garden Week of 1940, members of the Garden Club of Virginia visited the sanctuary, remarking that they "will take back ideas of the 'ideal' sanctuary," according to a project report.[51]

In the later years of the project, the sanctuary employed young people as guides through a New Deal youth program. Ray Daniels worked in this capacity for a few months in the spring of 1939. Ray and another young man were trained by a forewoman. "She'd tell us about the flowers and trees and we'd go on and repeat it. Then when

Log steps built by WPA workers in the Lee Park sanctuary, 1939. (The Library of Virginia.)

we got good enough, she'd let us go around ourselves. . . . There were a lot of flowers, and we had to remember all their names. They had such fancy names." The guides sat on a rustic bench near the entry to the sanctuary—"not a comfortable place to sit," Ray recalled—and greeted the visitors. On the slow days, he said, "we'd sit on the fence along the road and refresh ourselves about the flowers and go over our talks to ourselves." Ray especially remembered the day one visitor told him, "you must have been a good guide because you haven't stopped talking since we left." Talking about the birds was a more challenging task, he recalled, since "they wouldn't sit still."[52]

Donald Holden made a special effort to promote the sanctuary as a site for school and college field trips. During the first six weeks of school in 1936, more than 250 children visited. In 1940, Ralph Budd, a student at Patrick Copeland Elementary School in Hopewell, Virginia, wrote Donald: "Would it be all right if our class came to visit the 'bird Sanctuary' which you have in charge. We are trying to learn about birds in this part of Virginia." Donald answered, "We will be glad to have you visit. . . . We will try to have the birds at the feeding place, if you all will promise to keep real quiet."[53]

A Prototype for Other Sanctuaries

The Lee Park Sanctuary became a prototype for four similar WPA wildflower and bird sanctuaries in Virginia, also cosponsored by local garden clubs. Initiated between May 1937 and July 1938, the other projects were located in Charlottesville, Norfolk, Hopewell, and Danville. The Norfolk sanctuary, now the Norfolk Botanical Garden, took shape in 1937 in a large tract of woodlands anchored by a stand of loblolly pine. Charles Gillette, a Richmond landscape architect best known for designing dramatic gardens for Virginia country estates, helped to plan the Norfolk sanctuary, whose gardens today feature some of the most impressive displays of azaleas and camellias in the country. The Charlottesville sanctuary, a six-acre preserve within the city's McIntire Park, featured the "Rockery"—a rock garden dotted with violets, saxifrage, and Dutchman's-breeches. The supervisor of the McIntire project, Ruth Magness, hosted a nature talk show on a local radio station. The Hopewell site, built around a lake on the grounds of a municipal airport, attracted a multitude of wildlife, including eagles, red-winged blackbirds, and snapping turtles. Its brick Dutch oven was a popular location for fish fries and cookouts. The site was later sold to a private developer. The Danville sanctuary, the last to be constructed, was situated in an old cemetery. In 1939, the Garden Club of Virginia recognized the Danville project with its Massie Medal for outstanding preservation work, and this further encouraged Donald Holden to seek the same award for the Lee Park Herbarium Collection.[54]

Donald was appointed as a WPA consultant to these four other sanctuaries. She trained their staffs, advised on horticulture, and shared ideas for conservation and education. Staff from the other projects praised her work. "Mrs. Holden came to see us this month on the very first day," noted a 1938 report from the Charlottesville sanctuary. "The new ideas she brought us were startling at first, but how interesting they have proven to be." A later report from Charlottesville included this observation: "As usual, Mrs. Holden's stay was enjoyed, as well as being constructive. She gave the workers a talk which was very inspiring. She also instructed the Forewomen as to their responsibilities . . . Mrs. Holden can be such a help."[55]

Donald encouraged these other sanctuaries to document their accomplishments with their own herbaria. "In each sanctuary, the WPA workers have made a collection that is indeed worthy to be called a herbarium," she said in a 1939 radio broadcast.[56] (No vestige of these other collections has been found.)

For Donald, this expanded role as a consultant brought new opportunities to share her skills with a wider audience. But it also meant a heavier workload and substantial time away from home. Like any working mother, she struggled to balance her work and home responsibilities, and she sometimes had to go away at inopportune times—for example, when two of her sons had their tonsils taken out at the same time. Donald's mother, Annie, took care of the household, and just how much she contributed became obvious to Donald when Annie was out of town. "I've enjoyed housekeeping [while Annie was away], but I will be glad to turn the reins over to her," she wrote in a letter to Herbert. "How these modern women keep house, raise children and hold down a job is more than I can see. By night I can sleep like I'm dead."[57]

The End of the Lee Park Project

By late 1940, the WPA was winding down across the nation. In Petersburg the economy had picked up, and people were preparing for the possibility of war. "Everyone knew we were getting into the war," Ray Daniels recalled. "The parks just about closed down. The WPA closed down, people started working for the war industries, and people went off to war." Herbert Holden was among those who enlisted, joined later by his brother West. "It's almost time for me to give another son to dear old Uncle Sam," wrote Donald, "and my heartstrings are beginning to tighten."[58]

In November 1940, the Lee Park sanctuary received its final WPA allocation of $22,054. By that time, many of the WPA employees had already moved on. Donald took a supervisory job at a WPA sewing room, then switched again in late 1940 to a WPA records indexing project. "I went back to work to-day and was glad to get back," she wrote Herbert. "I don't like loafing, it does something to me." She never forgot what the New Deal had done for her, and remained a supporter of President Roosevelt. "To-day I'm going to Central Park to vote for Roosevelt. [Mother] already cast her vote for him."[59]

The Petersburg Garden Club sponsored and voluntarily tended the sanctuary for some years after WPA funding ceased. A 1943 chamber of commerce guide continued to list the bird and wildflower preserve as one of the main attractions of Lee Park—the last official mention that could be found.[60]

The lives of the women who worked in Lee Park took many different paths. Some, like Mary Webb Jones, did not survive the 1930s. In 1937, while still employed at the sanctuary, she contracted pneumonia and died; "she had been working out there in February in the cold weather," her daughter Marian recalled.[61]

For some women, life after the WPA was an ongoing struggle to make ends meet. In 1939, after being laid off, Catherine Johnson lived with her two children in a sparsely furnished three-room house on

Plum Street. She received six dollars a month in relief, and foraged wood from the riverbanks for heating and cooking. "Daily I walk the city streets trying to get work," she said in her oral history. She survived these lean years and stayed in Petersburg for at least some time after; in 1948 she was working as a stemmer for the Beach Tobacco Company.[62]

After leaving Lee Park, Mary Bell Focie held jobs with a tobacco company, as a private housekeeper, and as a home nurse. She raised a family, and one of her sons became the minister of a local Baptist church. "I know these feet have done some work," she said in 1998, in the kitchen of her house on Pegram Street. At age ninety-two, in fragile health, she still kept a memento from her WPA years: a rather delicate net mask that she wore in the WPA sewing room to filter out ambient fibers. "Everybody I worked with [on the WPA] has died," she said. In October 1998, Mary Bell died.[63]

In 1941, Donald Holden took a job as a hostess at Fort Lee in Petersburg. "Well here I am at the Service Club No 1. Camp Lee," she wrote to Herbert. "I worked Saturday, giving out games and information and talking to some of the boys who had just arrived, and were feeling a little low in spirits." Donald continued to juggle the demands of being a working mother. "I have been feeding my family on 50 cents a day per person, and the meals have been good too. I'm getting tired though, working and keeping house is no cinch." After the war, she took a job as a cafeteria manager for Bolling Junior High School. She maintained a garden of her own until almost the end of her life. "John and I planted four rows of onions yesterday," she wrote in a 1944 letter to Herbert. "My iris came so I planted that too. . . . I'll be glad to rest when I get home but I've got to plant the rest of the onions."[64]

Donald died of cancer at age sixty on June 3, 1950. Her mother, Annie Claiborne, outlived her by four years. The boxwoods from Donald's beloved Haldean Gardens, which she had transplanted to a rich plot at the Union Street house where the horse stable used to be, were passed down to Herbert. They became a defining feature of Herbert's garden, which he tended until his death in December 1998.

For many years after the war, Lee Park continued with few changes, except for some sales of land to private interests. But with the emergence of the Civil Rights movement, the park became a focal point of controversy over integration. In 1953, a group of black citizens filed a petition to integrate the swimming facilities at Willcox Lake. The city council resisted; rather than integrate, it closed the swimming area altogether. A federal judge indefinitely postponed a hearing on the petition, and the swimming area never reopened. Eventually the other recreation facilities were integrated.[65]

In addition to improving economic security for hundreds of thousands of women, the women's projects of the WPA helped to nudge forward societal perceptions about the kinds of jobs women could handle and the contributions they could make. The influence of the women's programs was perhaps most obvious at the highest administrative levels, where women like Ellen Woodward and Ella Agnew spoke out for women's rights and had a more significant impact on national policy than women had ever had before or would have for many years after.[66]

For most local women, like those in Petersburg, the progress toward workplace parity was slower and bumpier. Nevertheless, these women carried their families through hard times and showed fortitude in the face of adversity. Many saw their children go on to college, good jobs, or more stable futures. Their struggles and accomplishments did not go unappreciated. "Mother was not a down-in-the-dumps person," said Marian Baughman of her mother, Mary Webb Jones. "She would say, things are going to be better, reach for the stars"—an attitude that inspired Marian for the rest of her life. "Sometimes life turns out differently than you expect," Marian explained. "Sometimes a tragedy happens, but then it leads you down a path in life you never would have gone down."[67]

Lillian Anderson also knew tragedy—the baby she was carrying while working in the park had heart trouble and died at age five. Lillian's husband returned, and she did not go back to work. But Lillian never forgot her role in building the Lee Park sanctuary. Years later, her youngest daughter, Marion, sometimes took Girl Scouts on hikes through the woods along the old WPA trails. After these hikes, Marion explained, she would come back home and tell her mother about the pleasant trails and the pretty flowers. "And my mother would say, 'I know all that like the back of my hand. We did all of that.'"[68]

Preserving Virginia's Wildflower Treasures

A Fragile Botanical Wonderland

In June 1904, Roland M. Harper, a plant taxonomist from Alabama, gazed at the swiftly changing Virginia landscape from his seat aboard a passenger train clattering up the eastern seaboard. Seven miles south of Petersburg, near Burgess Station, Harper—an accomplished practitioner of the lost art of botanizing from the window of a moving train —glimpsed a patch of yellow-green in a meadowlike depression. As he looked more closely, his excitement grew. It was, unmistakably, a large colony of *Sarracenia flava*—hundreds upon hundreds of trumpets, their distinctive yellow funnels forming a bright rippled sea along the train tracks.[1]

Over the next forty years botanists from many states made pilgrimages to southeastern Virginia to see for themselves the many rare and interesting species that thrived in the boggy flats around Petersburg. Among the arrivals was Harvard's M. L. Fernald. Fernald's 1936 foray to Poo Run flat near Lee Park yielded ample rewards: "*Sarracenia flava* was, indeed, gratifyingly abundant and very handsome, with its stiffly erect slender yellow trumpets, but we were more interested in the carpet of the pink-flowered *Drosera capillaris* Poir.(unrecorded from north of South Carolina) upon which we walked." The next summer, after a two-mile trudge along railroad ties, Fernald finally set eyes upon the bog Harper had spotted from the train, but it was a mere vestige of its former splendor. "The railroad, with its high embankments and its culverts, has nearly ruined the *Sarracenia flava* area north of Burgess Station," Fernald wrote. "Only a few dilapidated plants persist."[2]

The conservation efforts of the 1930s helped to preserve several valuable sites but ultimately could not stave off the widespread destruction of priceless habitats. By the mid-1960s, the once-bountiful Poo Run flat, like numerous other sites in Virginia, had been wiped out. "Interstate 95 was bulldozed right through the flat," wrote botanist A. M. Harvill in a 1972 article, "and seemingly, to make sure that nothing escaped, the Earth was scraped down several feet, for several hundred yards on both sides of the highway, and used [for] fill material for the roadbed. Now, a few stunted loblolly pines and a scattering of other weeds grow on the desert-like surface of the deeply scraped mantle."[3]

Today a passenger gazing out a car window on I-85 in Petersburg, just below its junction with I-95, would never guess that behind a scrubby thicket, just a few hundred yards to the southeast, lay a pleasant park with an impressive array of native plant life. But unlike many formerly green spaces in the densely populated corridor south of Washington, D.C., the lands in and around Lee Park still shelter many of the species that Bessie Marshall painted. "The park has not been ruined," said Petersburg resident Garland Brockwell, as he stood above the dam at Willcox Lake, reminiscing about the days when he played there with Bessie Marshall's grandchildren.[4]

Lee Park Sixty Years after the WPA

Lee Park in the late 1990s is a wooded enclave of about 325 acres. Since the 1930s, the city of Petersburg has sold off parcels of park land to developers, private clubs, and the federal government. The park is bordered by residential and commercial development on the east and west, I-85 on the north, and the tracks of the Norfolk Southern (formerly Norfolk and Western) Railroad on the south. Black and

white residents use the athletic facilities and picnic tables, and the ball fields are host to national slow-pitch softball tournaments. But the rest of the park sees little activity, except for occasional botanical expeditions by students from Richard Bland College. Major sections lie secluded, well out of range of picnickers and softball players, accessible only to adventurous walkers.

A combination of factors has kept the park in this rather sleepy state. The era of diminished use began in the 1950s with the closing of the Willcox Lake swimming facilities. During the decades that followed, the city considered various proposals to renovate and expand the park's recreational facilities. In the 1970s, the city developed a fitness trail and made other improvements. More ambitious and costly proposals were shelved, including a 1976 plan to spend more than half

Lee Park in 1998, looking toward the south end of Willcox Lake. (Photograph by Will Kerner.)

a million dollars to create an elaborate recreation area with new athletic fields, bicycle trails, a boat-rental dock, and horse-show grounds.[5]

Meanwhile, the costs of maintaining, policing, and assuming liability for the more isolated sections of the park increased, and the city was having trouble keeping pace. There were reports of crime, vandalism, and other misconduct, and as fears mounted, park use declined. Heavy rains and snow caused mudslides on the hills, rendering some of the park trails unsafe. In an effort to reduce maintenance costs and safety concerns, the city chained off a section of the park road, preventing vehicles from looping through the secluded bottomland and rejoining the main road.[6]

While these decisions further decreased park use, they benefited plants and wildlife by keeping construction and pedestrian and car traffic to a minimum. Lee Park still contains most of the habitats found there in the 1930s. But the swamp habitats are largely gone, a victim of beaver dams and a rising lake level. Some meadow habitats are being lost to plant succession. Most of the open woodlands have been timbered, except for those on very steep slopes. The remaining habitats are also vulnerable. Erosion is one problem. Another threat is the proliferation of invasive alien species—kudzu, wisteria, Japanese honeysuckle, tree of heaven, and especially Japanese stilt grass, which has spread alarmingly.

Development is the most serious potential man-made threat. The city of Petersburg continues to struggle to maintain its economic base, putting pressure on local government to attract new business and find other sources of revenue. Selling park lands for development could become an appealing option, especially if the park is not meeting the needs of the community. Excessive timbering, gravel mining, road scraping, and imprudent or inadequate maintenance could also take a toll on plant life. These threats can be prevented, and some of the lost habitats restored, but it will take wise management, active planning, community support, and adequate funding.

The Wildflowers of Lee Park

The diversity of species in the herbarium collection raises exciting possibilities for botanical study in Lee Park. Forty-seven of the species in the collection have never been officially documented as occurring in Dinwiddie County.[7] Of the 295 species represented in the collection, about 64 percent—some 190 species—have been recently recorded or observed in Lee Park, including 2 relatively rare species, red milkweed (*Asclepias rubra*) and fern-leaved false foxglove (*Aureolaria pedicularia*).[8] It is likely that still more will be found.

The collection also contains seven species that are extremely rare or critically imperiled in Virginia: yellow colic-root, blue-hearts, spreading pogonia, white fringed orchis, trumpets, squarehead, and false asphodel. Seven other species represented are very rare or imperiled in Virginia: small whorled pogonia, red milkweed, grass-pink, rattlesnake-master, hairy pipewort, downy phlox (*Phlox pilosa*), and pitcher-plant (*Sarracenia purpurea*).[9]

The collection includes six southern species near the northern limits of their range in the eastern United States: pitcher-plant, squarehead, hairy pipewort, small black blueberry (*Vaccinium tenellum*), Carolina-lily, and rosin-weed. Four other species are near their northern limits in Virginia (although these also may occur as far north as New Jersey in the eastern part of their range): white fringed orchis, spreading pogonia, yellow colic-root, and false asphodel. Blazing star (*Liatris squarrosa*), downy phlox, Indian-physic, and rattlesnake-master are at or near their eastern limits in Virginia.[10]

Saving the Park and Its Habitats

Inspired by their predecessors of the 1930s, the members of the Petersburg Garden Club are working to preserve the wildflowers in Lee Park through a public and private partnership, not unlike the collaboration that built the first sanctuary. As a first step, they are seeking to register the park as a Virginia historic site. As long-term goals, they hope to gain city and community support to reopen some unused sections of the park, restore some of the trails, reclaim disappearing habitats, stop the spread of invasive species, and replant native species to prevent bank erosion. The club would like to see Lee Park once again become an outdoor classroom and laboratory, with environmentally sensitive recreational and educational programs for the entire Petersburg community.

In honor of Donald Holden, Bessie Marshall, and the other WPA workers, the club would some day like to develop a Holden-Marshall Memorial in Lee Park. "Bessie, Donald, and the other women here before us were the pioneers of the past, and their work should be preserved," said Bettie Guthrie, co-chair of the Herbarium Committee of the Petersburg Garden Club. "We're trying to be the pioneers of the future by working to reopen sections of Lee Park and offer an educational experience that will benefit all of Petersburg and all of Virginia."[11]

More than sixty years after their creation, Bessie Marshall's watercolors have energized a new cycle of preservation. With help from other people who appreciate the beauty of these illustrations and their real-life counterparts, the Petersburg Garden Club will be able to do further work to preserve the watercolors and ensure that the wildflower habitats of Lee Park do not go the way of Roland Harper's bog.

Notes

Introduction

1. The Garden Club of Virginia, "Historic Garden Week in Virginia, April 19–26, 1969," 52.

2. Many of the specimens represented in the collection were never painted, and some specimens appear to have been lost. In a small number of cases, the paintings were paired with specimens that had been misidentified or accidently switched. For example, the painting of butterfly pea depicts *Centrosema virginiana*, whereas the dried specimen is a different species of butterfly pea, *Clitoria mariana*.

3. Dorothy Caudle, interview by author, 11 February 1999.

4. Betty Steele, telephone conversation with author, 20 August 1998.

5. Samuel Robinson, interview by author, 18 May 1999.

6. A. M. Harvill, "The Tragic Fate of Poo Run," *Jeffersonia* 6, no. 4 (1972): 28.

7. See the afterword for a complete list of the species that are rare or imperiled or near their distributional limits.

8. Herbert Randall Holden, interview by author, 3 June 1998.

9. Donald Holden, "WPA Makes Possible Bird and Wild Flower Sanctuary at Petersburg," *W.P.A. Record* 1, no. 6 (March 1937): 1.

10. Robert Smart to D. Holden, 2 July 1937; H.R. Holden, interview.

11. D. Holden, "The Tie Up of the Petersburg Garden Club, the W.P.A., the Massey [*sic*] Medal," unpublished document for a Petersburg Garden Club meeting, 2 June 1948; H. R. Holden, interview.

12. D. Holden, "Tie Up."

13. D. Holden, "Tie Up"; Eleanor Boothe, presentation made at a meeting of the Garden Club of Virginia, 19 May 1948.

14. Anne Lewis, interview by author, 14 May 1998.

15. Katharine Heath to Betty Steele, 27 October 1995.

1. A Time of Social Change

1. Mary Bell (Goodwyn) Focie, interview by author, 13 May 1998.

2. Donald Holden, "Lee Park Sanctuary," *The Commonwealth* (July 1939): 22; "WPA Project in Lee Park Attracts Favorable Views," *Petersburg (Va.) Progress-Index,* 26 June 1939, 1.

3. "Sanctuary in Lee Park Made Haven for Wild Life," *Progress-Index,* 23 August 1936, 2; Ray Daniels, interview by author, 22 July 1998.

4. D. Holden, "WPA Makes Possible Bird and Wild Flower Sanctuary at Petersburg," *W.P.A. Record* 1, no. 6 (March 1937): 1.

5. Willcox Lake, named after the Willcox family of Petersburg, is today often referred to by the alternate spelling of Wilcox Lake. The original spelling, which was still prevalent in the 1930s, is used throughout this book.

6. Ronald L. Heinemann, *Depression and New Deal in Virginia: The Enduring Dominion* (Charlottesville: Univ. Press of Virginia, 1983), 16, 42; James G. Scott and Edward A. Wyatt IV, *Petersburg's Story* (Petersburg: Titmus Optical Co., 1960), 340–41; Focie, interview.

7. Martha H. Swain, *Ellen S. Woodward: New Deal Advocate for Women* (Jackson: Univ. Press of Mississippi, 1995), 54; Susan Ware, "Women and the New Deal," in *Fifty Years Later: The New Deal Evaluated,* ed. H. Sitkoff (New York: Knopf, 1985), reprinted in Melvyn Dubofsky and Stephen Burwood, eds., *Women and Minorities during the Great Depression* (New York: Garland, 1990), 124.

8. "795 Persons Employed by WPA Here," *Progress-Index,* 10 August 1936, 1.

9. Swain, *Woodward,* 1, 42–43; Sue Quinn, "Miss Ella Relates Story of Her Long Active Career in Pioneer Field," *Richmond Times-Dispatch,* 20 October 1944, 17.

10. Swain, *Woodward,* 49; Helen Hill Weed, "FERA-CWA-CWS," *American Journal of Nursing* 24 (March 1934): 183, cited in Swain, *Woodward,* 47.

11. "WPA Programs Important to Women Here," *Progress-Index,* 2 August 1936, 2; Heinemann, *Depression,* 91.

12. National Archives and Records Administrations II (NARA II), RG 69, Records of the Federal Emergency Relief Administration (FERA), Central correspondence, State series, Virginia 400, Emergency Relief Administration (Virginia), "Memo Regarding Women's Work," memorandum to superintendents of public welfare, 23 November 1933; Swain, *Woodward,* 46–47, 93; Jacqueline Jones, *Labor of Love, Labor of Sorrow* (New York: Vintage Books, 1985), 218–19.

13. NARA II, RG 69, Records of FERA, Central files, State series, Virginia 453, Virginia Women's Projects, letter from Ella Agnew to Frances Perkins, Secretary of Labor, 12 October 1933.

14. At least one bird and wildflower sanctuary project, and perhaps more,

had already been funded in Virginia through other New Deal programs. In a telegram dated 3 February 1934, Ella Agnew sent Ellen Woodward a list of the total number of women's FERA projects operating in the state; among them was a bird and wildflower sanctuary whose location was not specified. Also, in a letter dated 5 February 1934 to Eleanor Roosevelt, Ella Funk Myers of the *Richmond Times-Dispatch* asked Mrs. Roosevelt to endorse a proposal by the Richmond Federation of Garden Clubs to sponsor two bird and wildflower sanctuaries in that city's Forest Hill Park and Bryan Park with funds from the Civil Works Administration. If either program was started, it was apparently not continued with WPA funding; by 1937, neither site was listed as one of the WPA-funded wildflower sanctuaries in Virginia. See NARA II, RG 69, Records of FERA, Central files, State series, Virginia 453, Virginia Women's Projects.

15. Percilla Anderson, interview by author, 20 May 1999.

16. "WPA Projects Important to Women Here," *Progress-Index,* 2 August 1936, 2.

17. The habitat descriptions of the species in the herbarium collection were worded very much like those found in Merriman's manual, the reference of first resort for plant identification. Howard Smith, "Paul R. Merriman's Flora of Richmond," *Virginia Journal of Science* 25 (fall 1974): 132.

18. Jennie Jones, "The Orchidaceae in the Department of Agriculture Herbarium," n.d., Virginia Seed Laboratory; Clarence Williams, "Dr. John Dunn, a Virginia Botanist," *William and Mary Quarterly Historical Magazine,* 15 (April 1935): 110.

19. A. B. Massey, "Fernald, M. L., Midsummer Vascular Plants of Southeastern Virginia," *Claytonia* 2, nos. 8–9 (1936): 46; Edgar T. Wherry to Jennie Jones, 23 January 1930, Virginia Seed Laboratory.

20. Evie Bromley Key, "Virginia's Wildflower Sanctuaries," *Claytonia* 5, no. 3 (1939): 21.

21. Key, "Sanctuaries," 21.

22. D. Holden, "WPA Makes Possible," 1.

23. D. Holden, "Lee Park Sanctuary," 22.

24. Banister's wife, Martha Batte, was the widow of Abraham Jones, who held the first patent on the lands that eventually became Lee Park (Richard Jones, interview by author, 13 May 1998). One of the roads that today forms part of the western boundary of Lee Park is named Banister Road, presumably after the botanist's grandson, John Banister, a Revolutionary War colonel.

25. Joseph and Nesta Ewan, *John Banister and His Natural History of Virginia, 1678–1692* (Urbana: Univ. of Illinois Press, 1970), 40, 87, 107, 431–33.

26. Harriet Frye, *The Great Forest: John Clayton and Flora* (Hampton, Va.: Dragon Run Books, 1990), 40; A. M. Harvill, Jr., Charles E. Stevens, and Donna

M. E. Ware, *Atlas of the Virginia Flora* 1 (Farmville, Va.: Virginia Botanical Associates, 1977), 3–4; M. L. Fernald, "Local Plants of the Inland Coastal Plain, Part I," *Rhodora* 39 (September 1937): 326.

27. John Hendly Barnhardt, "Early Virginia Botany—Dr. James Greenway," *Claytonia* 1, no. 6 (1934): 54–55.

28. The Dimmock Line was named after Confederate Captain Charles H. Dimmock. The ravines above Willcox Lake were used for strategic forays during the Battles of Jerusalem Plank Road and Weldon Railroad.

29. When the Petersburg National Battlefield Park was created in 1927, the city of Petersburg conveyed to the National Park Service a twenty-four-acre slice of Lee Park land that contained the earthworks. In 1973, the federal government gave this land back to the city; at present it is part of Lee Park.

30. When the city first bought the watershed lands, they were part of Dinwiddie and Prince George Counties. They did not become part of the city of Petersburg until the 1921 annexation. City council minutes, city of Petersburg, 6 April 1893, 209, and 1 April 1895, 302.

31. City council minutes, city of Petersburg, 18 October 1921, 72, and 1 November 1921, 73; City Engineer, city of Petersburg, map of Lee Memorial Park, 1921.

32. *Report of the City of Petersburg for the Period September 15th, 1920 to June 30th, 1923,* 81–82; Samuel Robinson, interview by author, 18 May 1999.

33. D. Holden, "Broadcast, March 3, Wild Flower and Bird Sanctuary," unpublished notes from a radio program, n.d.

34. Emily Dinwiddie, "The Committee on Flora of Richmond and Vicinity," *Claytonia* 1, no. 2 (1934): 5.

35. *Art for the Millions* was the title of a compilation of essays by the administrators and artists of the Federal Art Project. See Francis V. O'Connor, ed., *Art for the Millions* (Greenwich, Conn.: New York Graphic Society, 1973).

36. Jonathan Harris, *Federal Art and National Culture: The Politics of Identity in New Deal America* (Cambridge: Cambridge Univ. Press, 1995), 44, 85.

2. Bessie Niemeyer Marshall

1. Garland Brockwell, interview by author, 30 March 1998.

2. Jane Hix, "Leading Publications Use Work of Portsmouth Artist," *Portsmouth (Va.) Star,* 29 April 1951, A8.

3. J. B. Jackson, interview by author, 30 March 1998.

4. Louise Niemeyer Fontaine and Lewis Kirby, *Tidewater Ancestors* (Petersburg, Va.: L. Kirby and Plummer Printing Co., 1991), xiii–xiv.

5. Helen Marshall Fedziuk, interview by author, 30 March 1998; Fontaine and Kirby, *Tidewater,* xiv.

6. Gladys Marshall, telephone conversation with author, 15 June 1998; Katharine Fontaine Heath to Betty Steele, 27 October 1995.

7. Letter from Bruce Marshall to author, 7 April 1998.

8. Elizabeth Nash MacKenzie, interview by author, 30 March 1998.

9. Fedziuk, "Biography and Reflections," unpublished recollections, n.d.

10. Elizabeth Marshall Digges, telephone conversation with author, 1 June 1998.

11. Fedziuk, interview by Betty Steele and Bettie Guthrie, 30 August 1993.

12. Fedziuk, interview, 30 March 1998.

13. "Petersburg Garden Club Closes Successful Year," *Progress Index,* 14 March 1937, 2.

14. Fedziuk, interview, 30 March 1998.

15. Hix, "Leading Publications," A8.

16. Bessie Marshall, unpublished notebook, 1938-1940.

17. Herbert Randall Holden, interview by author, 3 June 1998; G. Marshall, conversation.

18. The paintings of the small whorled pogonia have characteristics which suggest Bessie Marshall may have painted them from dried specimens.

19. B. Marshall, notebook.

20. Donald Holden, excerpt from unpublished date book, April 1947.

21. Fedziuk, telephone conversation with author, 15 July 1998.

22. The discussion in this section of Bessie Marshall's technique as an artist was informed by interviews conducted by Betty Steele, Bettie Guthrie, and the author with Boots Holden, 31 March 1998; Judy Gilman, 22 July 1998; and Merri Nelson, 21 September 1998.

23. Digges, telephone conversation.

24. Louise Marshall McCrensky to H. Fedziuk, December 1994.

25. B. Marshall to Catherine Marshall, 13 March 1938.

26. D. Holden, unpublished note, n.d.; B. Marshall, notebook; B. Marshall to H. Fedziuk, 17 April 1940.

27. B. Marshall to C. Marshall, 13 November 1938.

28. B. Marshall to C. Marshall, 13 November 1938; B. Marshall to H. Fedziuk, 2 November 1939.

29. Wellmer Pessels, Macmillan Company, to B. Marshall, 28 July 1939; B. Marshall to H. Fedziuk, 5 October 1939.

30. Letter from E. C. L. Miller to B. Marshall, 5 October 1940; letter from H. L. Blomquist to B. Marshall, 13 March 1941.

31. B. Marshall to H. Fedziuk, 7 November 1940.

32. B. Marshall to H. Fedziuk, 7 November 1940; *House and Garden,* September 1941, 10; B. Marshall to H. Fedziuk, 28 October 1941.

33. Frank Fisher, *National Geographic,* to B. Marshall, 26 December 1944;

M. McKay, *Encyclopedia Britannica,* to B. Marshall, 29 January 1945, 6 March 1945; B. Marshall to Arthur (Pinky) Marshall, n.d.

34. B. Marshall to H. Fedziuk, 6 March 1945; L. McCrensky, to H. Fedziuk; H. Fedziuk to Betty Steele, 1 May 1992.

35. B. Marshall to H. Fedziuk, 10 January 1945; Walter Weber, wildlife artist, to B. Marshall, 23 November 1945.

36. B. Marshall to H. Fedziuk, 20 January 1944 and 29 January 1945.

37. Colgate Darden to B. Marshall, 17 January 1948.

38. H. Fedziuk, letter to author, 4 April 1998.

39. Bruce Marshall, letter to author.

40. Elizabeth Nash MacKenzie, interview by author, 30 March 1998.

41. Digges, telephone conversation; H. Fedziuk, letter to author, 4 April 1998.

42. Richard Marshall, interview by Betty Steele and Bettie Guthrie, 30 August 1993; Heath to Steele.

3. The WPA Wildflower and Bird Sanctuary

Much of the information in this chapter has been informed by the unpublished papers of Donald Holden; by articles from the *Petersburg (Va.) Progress-Index;* and by monthly reports (March 1937 to May 1939) submitted by the Virginia WPA wildflower sanctuary projects to the WPA Women's Work Division in Richmond, held in the National Archives and Records Administration II (NARA II), RG 69, Records of the Works Progress Administration (WPA), Records of the Division of Professional and Service Projects, 1935–1941, State narrative reports, Virginia.

1. Mary Webb Jones, journal, n.d.

2. "Local WPA Work Shown Here," *Progress-Index,* 24 April 1936, 1; "Sanctuary in Lee Park Is Made Haven for Wild Life," *Progress-Index,* 23 August 1936, 2.

3. Marian Jones Baughman, telephone conversation with author, 15 September 1998.

4. Percilla Anderson, interview by author, 20 May 1999; Marion Anderson, interview by author, 20 May 1999.

5. D. Holden, "Lee Park Wild Flower and Bird Sanctuary," unpublished report written for the Petersburg Chamber of Commerce, 13 May 1938.

6. The total project funding was estimated by adding the allocations shown on all available project file indices for this project from November 1935 through November 1940, at NARA II, RG 69, Index to the WPA project files, microfilm T-935 through T-937, Virginia, City of Petersburg, O.P. 65-31-2639, 165-31-7315, 665-31-3-249? (illegible), 665-31-3-26? (illegible), and 165-1-31-187? (illegible), and by announcements of additional WPA allocations in the *Progress-Index,* 7 December 1935, 28 May 1936, 21 February 1937, and 28 January 1938.

7. D. Holden, "The Tie Up of the Petersburg Garden Club, the W.P.A., the Massey [*sic*] Medal," unpublished document written for a meeting of the Petersburg Garden Club, 2 June 1948; "Planting of Dogwood Trees at Wilcox Lake Is Assured," *Progress-Index,* 28 February 1936, 1, 7; Donald Holden, "WPA project 65-31-2369, Bird and Flower Sanctuary," unpublished document, n.d.

8. NARA II, RG 69, Records of the WPA, Civil Works Administration project files, Virginia, microfilm E-531 (A3112, roll 6255) and E-531 (reel 20); NARA II, RG 79, Records of the National Park Service, Records of the Branch of Recreation, Land Planning, and State Cooperation, narrative reports concerning Civilian Conservation Corps projects in National Park Service areas, MP-2, Petersburg National Battlefield, October 1934.

9. Frances Johnson, interview by author, 3 March 1998; D. Holden to Herbert Randall Holden, 25 November 1940.

10. John Herbert Claiborne, *Seventy-Five Years in Old Virginia* (New York: Neale Publishing, 1904), 133, 200.

11. Herbert Randall Holden, interview by author, 3 June 1998.

12. "Miss Claiborne Now Bride of S. W. Holden," *Progress-Index,* 11 June 1915.

13. D. Holden to H. R. Holden, 5 May 1941.

14. "West Holden Dies at Home," *Progress-Index,* 8 July 1933, 1; Frank Myers, interview by author, 14 May 1998; H. R. Holden, interview; D. Holden to H. R. Holden, 10 April 1941.

15. Helen Doyle Holden, interview, 3 June 1998; Myers, interview.

16. H. R. Holden, interview.

17. "Bird Preserve in Spotlight," *Progress-Index,* 25 September 1936, 15.

18. No list of employees has been found among local records or state or national archives, although some names are known from project reports, oral histories, and interviews with Petersburg residents. Other attempts to locate surviving employees turned up only one person, Mary Bell (Goodwyn) Focie, who died in October 1998.

19. D. Holden, "Bird and Wild Flower Sanctuary," unpublished document, 20 October 1936; NARA II, Index to WPA project files; D. Holden, "Lee Park Bird and Wild Flower Sanctuary," unpublished document, spring 1939.

20. NARA II, WPA monthly reports, March 1937–May 1939; D. Holden, "Project 65-31-2369."

21. Jacqueline Jones, *Labor of Love, Labor of Sorrow* (New York: Vintage Books, 1985), 217–19; Harvard Sitkoff, *A New Deal for Blacks* (New York: Oxford Univ. Press, 1978), 44–45; Roger Biles, *The South and the New Deal* (Lexington: University of Kentucky, 1994), 115; Ronald L. Heinemann, *Depression and New Deal in Virginia: The Enduring Dominion* (Charlottesville: Univ. Press of Virginia, 1983), 99.

22. Susie R. C. Byrd was a college-educated African-American woman from Petersburg who was employed in the 1930s by the WPA Writers' Project to interview former slaves, write life histories of black Virginians, and document economic conditions in the black community.

23. Susie R. C. Byrd, interviews with Catherine Johnson, 20 February 1939, and Minnie Price, 30 January 1939, from the Hampton University archives, in the Kevin Barry Perdue Archive of Traditional Culture, University of Virginia.

24. Mary Webb Jones, WPA reassignment slip, 30 November 1935; Carrie McNear, interview by author, 20 May 1999; Byrd, interview with Allie Jones, 27 February 1939, Kevin Barry Perdue Archive of Traditional Culture, University of Virginia.

25. Mary Bell Focie, interview by author, 13 May 1998; NARA II, WPA monthly report, July 1938; D. Holden, "Project 65-31-2369."

26. The documents and maps of the period give varying figures for the total acreage in Lee Park, anywhere from about 500 acres to about 1,500 acres. The city owned a considerable buffer of undeveloped land around the park, some of which was used to create a public golf course, and the discrepancies may stem from whether these buffer lands, including the golf-course land, were considered part of the actual park.

27. D. Holden, "WPA Makes Possible Bird and Wild Flower Sanctuary at Petersburg," *W.P.A. Record* 1, no. 6 (March 1937): 1.

28. The judgment about which plants failed to thrive was probably premature, since it would take at least two years of consecutive blooming to know.

29. Samuel Robinson, interview by author, 18 May 1999.

30. NARA II, WPA monthly reports, December 1937, February 1939.

31. Ray Daniels, interview by author, 22 July 1998; H. R. Holden, interview.

32. "WPA Conservation Work," *Progress-Index,* 25 June 1939. Japanese honeysuckle was known even then to be an invasive species, but perhaps the city and the project supervisors felt the need for erosion control outweighed this concern.

33. Focie, interview.

34. Robinson, interview; Focie, interview.

35. P. Anderson, interview.

36. Byrd, C. Johnson interview.

37. Byrd, M. Price interview.

38. P. Anderson, interview; Focie, interview.

39. NARA II, WPA monthly reports, December 1937, January 1938; D. Holden, "Bird," Oct. 1936.

40. Robinson, interview.

41. D. Holden, "WPA Makes Possible," 1; D. Holden, "Broadcast, March 3, Wild Flower and Bird Sanctuary," unpublished notes for radio program, n.d.

42. Floristic studies currently being conducted in Lee Park by Donna M. E. Ware suggest that at least some of the plants in the sanctuary may have been transplanted into soil that was too acidic or sandy—for example, *Hepatica americana, Galearis spectabilis,* and *Cercis canadensis.*

43. NARA II, WPA monthly report, July 1938.

44. M. L. Fernald to D. Holden, 27 April 1939.

45. D. Holden, "Project 65-31-2369"; NARA II, WPA monthly report, May 1938; D. Holden, "Lee Park Sanctuary," *The Commonwealth* (July 1939): 22.

46. "Public Is Requested Not to Pick Flowers in Beautified Area," *Progress-Index,* 6 April 1936, 1.

47. D. Holden, "Project 65-31-2369"; NARA II, WPA monthly reports, September 1937, December 1937; D. Holden, "WPA Makes Possible," 2.

48. D. Holden, "Broadcast"; D. Holden, "Wild Flowers That Should Not Be Destroyed," unpublished paper, n.d.; NARA II, WPA monthly reports, January 1939, March 1938.

49. M. Jones, journal.

50. NARA II, WPA monthly reports, October 1937, October 1938.

51. NARA II, RG 69, Records of the WPA, Records of the Division of Professional and Service Projects, State narrative reports, Virginia, project attendance report, 27 May 1940; D. Holden, "Bird," Oct. 1936; NARA II, WPA monthly report, December 1937.

52. Daniels, interview.

53. D. Holden, "Bird," Oct. 1936; Ralph Budd to D. Holden, 15 April 1940, with response from D. Holden at bottom.

54. NARA II, WPA monthly reports, March 1937–May 1939; George C. Longest, *Genuis in the Garden* (Richmond: Virginia State Library, 1992), 129; D. Holden, "Tie Up."

55. NARA II, WPA monthly reports, February 1938, June 1938.

56. D. Holden, "Broadcast."

57. D. Holden to H. R. Holden, 19 September 1944.

58. Daniels, interview; H. R. Holden, interview.

59. NARA II, Index to WPA project files, microfilm T-937, Virginia, city of Petersburg, O.P. 165-1-31-187? (illegible); D. Holden to H. R. Holden, 31 December 1940, 3 November 1940.

60. Petersburg Chamber of Commerce, "Places of Historical Interest" (1943).

61. Baughman, telephone conversation.

62. Byrd, C. Johnson interview; Nancy J. Martin-Perdue and Charles L. Perdue, *Talk about Trouble* (Chapel Hill: Univ. of North Carolina Press, 1996), 199.

63. Focie, interview.

64. D. Holden to H. R. Holden, 12 August 1941, 21 September 1944, 18 October 1944.

65. "Council Asked to Open Willcox Lake to Negroes," *Progress-Index,* 8 July 1953, 1; "Willcox Lake Not to Open for Public Use This Year," *Progress-Index,* 13 March 1954, 1; council minutes, city of Petersburg, 19 October 1954, 476; "City Will Not Open Willcox Lake Next Year," *Progress-Index,* 20 October 1954.

66. Susan Ware, "Women and the New Deal," in Harvard Sitkoff, ed., *Fifty Years Later: The New Deal Evaluated* (New York: Alfred A. Knopf, 1985), reprinted in Melvyn Dubofsky and Stephen Burwood, eds., *Women and Minorities during the Great Depression* (New York: Garland, 1990), 333–34, 339; Anthony J. Badger, *The New Deal* (London: Macmillan Education, 1989), 256.

67. Baughman, telephone conversation.

68. M. Anderson, interview.

Afterword

1. Roland M. Harper, "*Sarracenia flava* in Virginia," *Torreya* 4 (1904): 123.

2. M. L. Fernald, "Local Plants of the Inland Coastal Plain, Part I," *Rhodora* 39 (September 1937), 326; M. L. Fernald, "Noteworthy Plants of Southeastern Virginia," *Rhodora* 40 (October 1938), 368.

3. A. M. Harvill, "The Tragic Fate of Poo Run," *Jeffersonia* 6, no. 4 (1972): 28.

4. Garland Brockwell, interview by author, 30 March 1998.

5. Raymond, Parish, Pine, and Plavnick, community development consultants, "Willcox Lake Recreation Area Report," report to the city of Petersburg, 1976.

6. Guthrie Smith, director of public works, city of Petersburg, telephone conversation with author, 27 July 1998; Dulaney Ward, planning office, city of Petersburg, interview by author, 31 March 1998.

7. Floristic records are listed by county, not city. Plant distributions are based on A. M. Harvill Jr., et al. *Atlas of the Virginia Flora,* 3d ed. (Burkeville, Va.: Virginia Botanical Assoc., 1992).

8. In 1998, Donna M. E. Ware began a study of the vascular flora (ferns, conifers, and flowering plants) of Lee Park and the entire watershed of Willcox Branch. As of June 1999, she had documented approximately 550 species, of which approximately 190 are represented in the herbarium collection.

9. The first seven species are listed as being extremely rare or critically imperiled by Natural Heritage Resources of Virginia, meaning that they have five or fewer occurrences or very few remaining individuals in Virginia, or are otherwise vulnerable to extirpation in Virginia. The next eight are very rare or imperiled,

with six to twenty occurrences or few remaining individuals in Virginia, or otherwise vulnerable to extirpation.

10. The six species near their overall northern limits have been rarely or never documented (0 to 3 county records) north of the James River. The other species have been documented in a significantly limited number of counties north of the James River. Ranges are based on Harvill et al., 1992, and on Henry A. Gleason and Arthur Cronquist, *Manual of Vascular Plants of the Northeastern United States and Adjacent Canada,* 2d ed. (Bronx, New York: New York Botanical Garden, 1991).

11. Bettie Guthrie, interview by author, 29 September 1998.

PART TWO

The Watercolors of the Lee Park Herbarium Collection

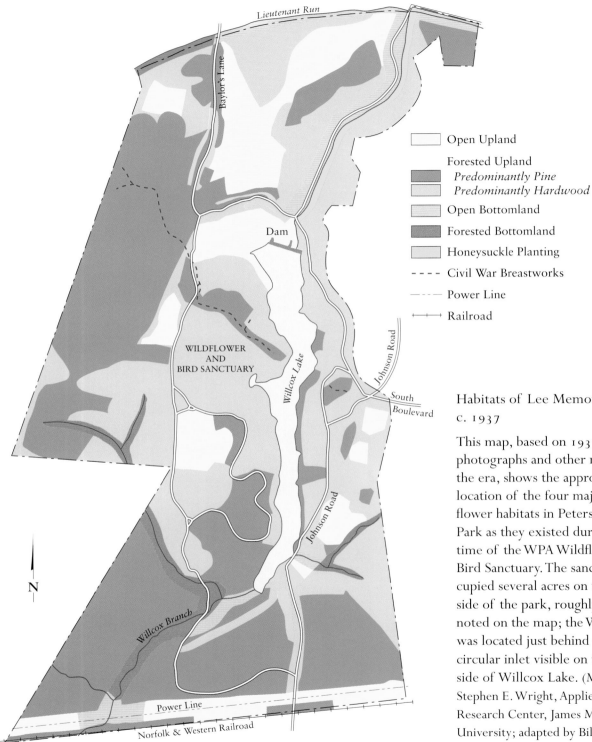

Lieutenant Run

Baylor's Lane

Dam

WILDFLOWER
AND
BIRD SANCTUARY

Willcox Lake

Johnson Road

South
Boulevard

Johnson Road

Willcox Branch

N

Power Line

Norfolk & Western Railroad

Open Upland

Forested Upland
Predominantly Pine
Predominantly Hardwood

Open Bottomland

Forested Bottomland

Honeysuckle Planting

- - - Civil War Breastworks

—··— Power Line

++++ Railroad

Habitats of Lee Memorial Park,
c. 1937

This map, based on 1937 aerial
photographs and other maps of
the era, shows the approximate
location of the four major wildflower habitats in Petersburg's Lee
Park as they existed during the
time of the WPA Wildflower and
Bird Sanctuary. The sanctuary occupied several acres on the west
side of the park, roughly where
noted on the map; the WPA bog
was located just behind the large
circular inlet visible on the west
side of Willcox Lake. (Map by Dr.
Stephen E. Wright, Applied Spatial
Research Center, James Madison
University; adapted by Bill Nelson.)

Arrangement of Illustrations by Habitat

Bessie Marshall painted 238 watercolors for the Lee Park Herbarium Collection. Almost all of them are reproduced here, except for a few that are near-duplicates of other paintings in the collection. As shown on the map on the facing page, Lee Park in the late 1930s had four main habitats—open upland, forested upland, open bottomland, and forested bottomland. The illustrations are arranged here according to the *primary* habitat of the species depicted (some grew in more than one habitat in the park).

The majority of the common and botanical names used here are the same as those that appear on the original labels of the herbarium collection. When necessary, the names have been changed to correct misidentifications, avoid confusion between two species with the same common name, or update old nomenclature that has fallen out of favor.

The scientific nomenclature used here is based on Flora of North America Editorial Committee, *Flora of North America, Vol. 3: Magnolio-phyta / Magnoliopsida: Magnoliidae and Hamamelidae* (New York: Oxford Univ. Press, 1997); Henry A. Gleason and Arthur Cronquist, *Manual of Vascular Plants of Northeastern United States and Adjacent Canada,* 2d ed. (New York: New York Botanical Garden, 1991); John T. Kartesz, *A Synonymized Checklist of the Vascular Flora of the United States, Canada, and Greenland* (Portland, Ore.: Timber Press, 1994); A. E. Radford, H. E.

Ahles, and C. R. Bell, *Manual of the Vascular Flora of the Carolinas* (Chapel Hill: Univ. of North Carolina Press, 1968); and Virginia Division of Natural Heritage, *Ecoflora: Abbreviated Checklist, June 1999* (Richmond, Va.: Department of Conservation and Recreation, 1999).

Open Upland

Most of the open or partly shaded upland in Lee Park is on the west side, atop a plateau about 165 feet in elevation. The main park road runs southward through this open area, passing a picnic pavilion on the east, Civil War breastworks on both sides, and a ball field on the west. Surrounding the ball field are mowed fields where one finds sweet vernal grass, Bermuda grass, wild field-pansies, small bluets, and other wildflowers. In the 1930s, a car could travel the entire length of the park road, but a chain now blocks access to its southern section, right before the road forks into two branches that later meet to form a loop.

Just beyond the fork in the road lies a meadow of about three acres. In the WPA days, the meadow was an open field sometimes used for field hockey. In later years, pines began taking over, threatening to shade out the meadow flowers. If left to its own devices, the meadow would quickly become pine woods. Recently the city of Petersburg has begun to clear the meadow periodically, and herbaceous annuals and perennials have come back in mass, including some of the more eye-catching species that Bessie Marshall painted. Two unusual grasses also grow in the meadow: fall witchgrass and a short-leaved beard grass that glimmers a rosy color in the early morning dew.

Beyond the meadow, the road passes through forested upland, but the road banks are still open enough to provide a habitat for bird's-foot violet, American feverfew, and other wildflowers.

Just north of the railroad tracks that form the park's southern boundary is the treeless swath of a power-line cut, which already existed in the 1930s. At some later point, bulldozers worked over this area, and the older power line was replaced with bigger pylons. The eastern part of this upland plateau is a junglelike thicket of sumac and blackberry, with some low moist pockets that favor rushes, panic grasses, and poison ivy. But one still finds mountain-mint, blazing star, and other interesting wildflowers here. The western part of the swath is less tangled with overgrowth; here wild strawberry, dewberry, several kinds of goldenrod, and Indian grass proliferate. Tree of heaven, an introduced species, has invaded a portion of the power-line right-of-way.

WILD STRAWBERRY

Fragaria virginiana Duchesne

People and other animals enjoy the sweet berries of this parent of the modern cultivated strawberry. The yellow cone in the middle of each flower matures into a single fleshy strawberry, with tiny seedlike fruits embedded in its surface. The Romans named the strawberry "fraga" because of its delightful fragrance.

B. N. Marshall

BIRD'S-FOOT VIOLET
Viola pedata L.

Bessie Marshall's Victorian nosegay of bird's-foot violet illustrates the two different genetic color forms of the species—the roosters and the hens—in various stages of bloom. The "rooster" has two dark violet petals on top, while the "hen" has uniformly light violet petals. The roosters and hens grow on different plants. In both forms, a little orange beak of stamens pokes out from the flat-faced flower.

ROSE-PINK

Sabatia angularis (L.) Pursh

DWARF IRIS

Iris verna L.

BUTTERFLY-WEED
Asclepias tuberosa L.

AMERICAN FEVERFEW
Parthenium integrifolium L.

B.N. Marshall

ROSIN-WEED
Silphium compositum Michx.

Growing along roadsides and in the power-line swath of Lee Park, rosin-weed approaches its northern limit in the coastal plain. This plant may tower up to nine feet tall, and its stem, when cut, oozes resinous juice. Abundant colonies of rosin-weed once grew near Petersburg, but botanists did not discover them until the late nineteenth century—which showed how little botanical work had been done in the region, for this huge plant could scarcely have gone unnoticed.

GREEN MILKWEED
Asclepias viridiflora Raf.

Smaller than some other milkweeds, the green milkweed blooms in early August in Lee Park. Its flowers, like those of several other species of milkweed, grow in tight clusters that relax somewhat as they mature. The inset shows a single flower with five light-colored anther wings at the tip, five green hoods pressed upward, and green petals pushed back against the stalk. As pictured here, the stem typically leans over sideways.

B.N.Marshall

CLASPING-LEAVED MILKWEED
Asclepias amplexicaulis Sm.

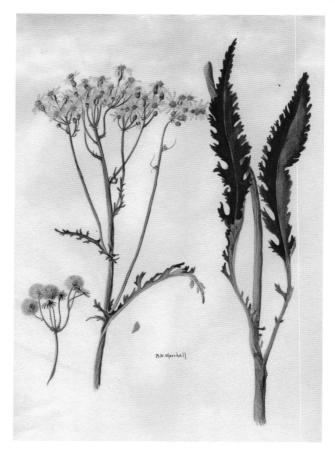

SMALL'S SQUAW-WEED
Senecio anonymus Wood

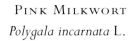

CURTISS' *or* PURPLE MILKWORT
Polygala curtissii Gray

PINK MILKWORT
Polygala incarnata L.

B.M.Marshall

Leopard's-Bane
Arnica acaulis (Walt.) B.S.P.

This knee-high plant, which grows in the Lee Park meadow and around the Civil War breastworks, has a hairy stem and an ample rosette of ground-hugging leaves. Long ray flowers with notched tips encircle a central disk of small, five-lobed tubular flowers. Also shown here are a dandelion-like puff of fruits and a single fruit with its fuzzy, parachute-like pappus.

COLIC-ROOT
Aletris farinosa L.

Bessie Marshall's sectional rendering of this waist-high plant captures its warty-textured flowers ("farinosa" means mealy) and sassy orange stamens. In 1936, in a pastured corner of the Poo Run bog near Petersburg, Harvard botanist M. L. Fernald came upon a patch of *A. farinosa* growing alongside its less common relative, yellow colic-root, *A. aurea,* which Bessie Marshall also painted. In the midst of this patch, Fernald noticed two curious plants—apparently hybrids between these two—which luckily, he observed, had been spared by the cows grazing nearby.

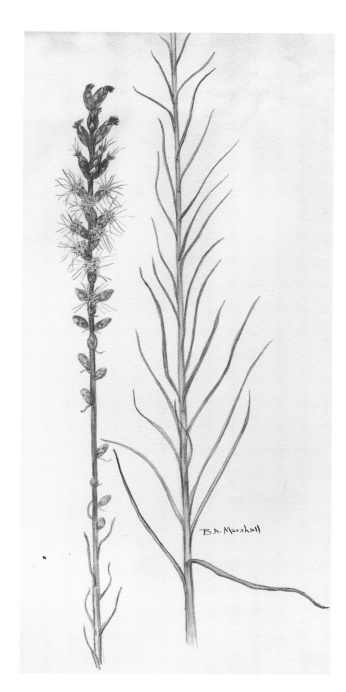

SAMPSON'S SNAKEROOT
Orbexilum pedunculatum (P. Mill.) Rydb.

BLAZING STAR *or* BUTTON SNAKEROOT
Liatris spicata (L.) Willd.

SILVER ASTER
Aster concolor L.

WHITE-TOPPED ASTER
Sericocarpus asteroides (L.) B.S.P.

NARROW-LEAVED
WHITE-TOPPED ASTER
Sericocarpus linifolius (L.) B.S.P.

STIFF-LEAVED ASTER
Ionactis linariifolius (L.) Greene

DOWNY LOBELIA
Lobelia puberula Michx.

LARGER *or* HYSSOP SKULLCAP
Scutellaria integrifolia L.

HAIRY SKULLCAP

Probably an extreme form of *Scutellaria elliptica* Muhl. ex Spreng.

B. N. Marshall

GOAT'S RUE
Tephrosia virginiana (L.) Pers.

Goat's rue has a distinctive bicolored flower, with pink side petals and a contrasting yellow-green banner petal. Its pinnate leaves culminate in one odd leaflet at the tip. This species requires highly acidic soils and will die when transplanted. It also contains a substance that some Indian tribes used as a fish poison.

Blazing Star

Liatris squarrosa (L.) Michx.

Graceful wands of blazing star
are a welcome sight in the open
upland of Lee Park, where this
species approaches its eastern
limit in Virginia. The rose-purple
"flowers" are actually clusters
of tubular flowers, each with a
forked style that seems to flicker
out like a snake's tongue, inviting pollination. In 1936, botanist
M. L. Fernald collected a specimen of *L. squarrosa* for his
herbarium at Harvard University in sandy soil south of
Petersburg.

B.N. Marshall—

B.N. Marshall

PRAIRIE WILLOW
Salix humilis Marsh.

The silky catkins of the prairie willow, or small pussy willow, appear in late winter in open areas and woodland margins of Lee Park. The catkin type shown here is a mass of simple male flowers. (Fruit-bearing female catkins would appear on a separate plant.) Each male flower consists of two stamens, which are couched in a dark scale bearing long hairs—the feline-like "fur." As the stamens mature, they split and release yellow pollen. The immature stamens, which are red, are visible on the branch at the right.

SUNDROPS
Oenothera fruticosa L. ssp. *glauca* (Michx.) Strahley

NARROW-LEAVED SUNDROPS
Oenothera fruticosa L. ssp. *fruticosa*

MARYLAND GOLDEN ASTER
Chrysopsis mariana (L.) Ell.

The golden color of these ray flowers is a cue that this species is not a true aster. Here Bessie Marshall shows some central disk flowers in bud and others already opened. In the open flowers, one can see the styles and anthers, as well as the bristly tufts that emanate from the top of each ovary. The spatula-shaped leaves have a thick whitened rib up the middle.

NARROW-LEAVED MOUNTAIN-MINT
Pycnanthemum tenuifolium Schrad.

WILD PLUM
Probably *Prunus angustifolia* Marsh.

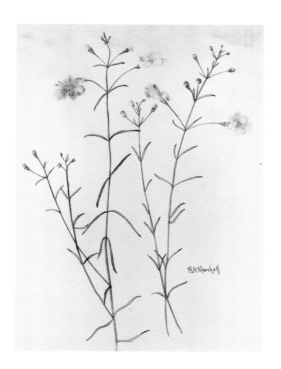

BLUNT-LEAVED FALSE FOXGLOVE
Probably *Agalinis obtusifolia* Raf.

SCOTCH BROOM
Cytisus scoparius (L.) Link

ELEPHANT'S FOOT
Elephantopus tomentosus L.

FIELD-THISTLE
Cirsium discolor (Muhl. ex Willd.) Spreng.

This common native thistle blooms in autumn in the fields and waste places of Lee Park. The flowers that form the thistle head issue from a cup-shaped mass of spine-tipped bracts. The spiny leaves have a woolly mat of white hairs on the underside. The Lee Park Herbarium Collection contains a specimen (but no watercolor) of a cousin, the Virginia-thistle (*C. virginianum*), which is very rare in Virginia.

B. A. Marshall

LARGE-FLOWERED ASTER
Aster grandiflorus L.

Recorded only in Virginia and North Carolina, this late-blooming aster has the most limited range of any species in the Lee Park Herbarium Collection. But unlike some other species with a narrow range, these plants grow in abundance—making a splendid sight, with their large heads, purplish ray flowers, and small, firm leaves. Vases filled with large-flowered asters decorated the WPA sanctuary exhibit at the 1937 Petersburg fair.

BLACK-EYED SUSAN
Rudbeckia hirta L.

Bessie Marshall chose to illustrate this favorite native flower in profile. The "eye" of the flower is actually a conelike structure dotted with purple-black tubular florets. The leaves and stalk are covered with eyelash-like hairs. In colonial Virginia, travelers rubbed down their horses after a long ride with crumpled stalks of black-eyed Susan.

SMALL WHITE MORNING-GLORY

Ipomoea lacunosa L.

This is a rare pink-flowered variant of a species that usually has white flowers.

(facing page)

COMMON MORNING-GLORY

Ipomoea purpurea (L.) Roth

An ornamental plant from tropical America that became naturalized, this fast-growing vine twines around anything in its way. This species of morning-glory has several different genetic color forms and usually has heart-shaped leaves. The flowers bloom in early morning and close by afternoon. Here Bessie Marshall has shown the tightly furled buds, the full flowers, and the withering blossoms.

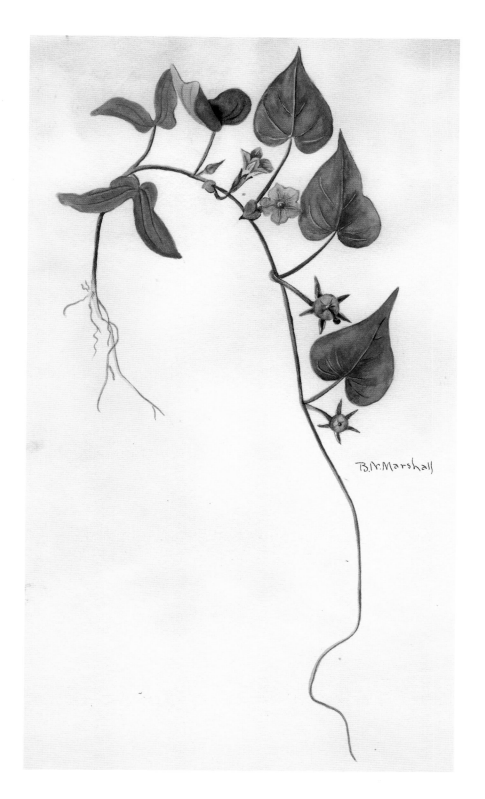

B.M.Marshall

IVY-LEAVED MORNING-GLORY
Ipomoea hederacea Jacq.

The sepals of this hairy species have tail-like tips, depicted here. The dried specimen that was mistakenly paired with this painting in the Lee Park Herbarium Collection was actually a specimen of *I. purpurea* that had three-lobed leaves instead of its typical heart-shaped leaves.

WOOLLY BLUE VIOLET
Viola sororia Willd. (smooth-stemmed variant)

BOUNCING BET
Saponaria officinalis L.

WILD POTATO-VINE
Ipomoea pandurata (L.) G. F. W. Mey.

Wild potato-vine trails along the sandy roadway near the Lee Park meadow. Man-of-the-earth is another name for this species—an allusion to its large tuberlike root, which can grow to a depth of three feet and can weigh several pounds. In this composition, Bessie Marshall has left ample white background space to accentuate the gracefulness of the plant.

B. N. Marshall

FIVE-FINGER
Potentilla canadensis L.

Five-finger needs plenty of light to produce its bright yellow flowers. Also known as cinquefoil, this low, spreading plant has leaves with five leaflets. Bessie Marshall sent this painting to *Encyclopedia Britannica* when she sought a commission to draw wildflowers for the junior edition.

PARTRIDGE-PEA
Chamaecrista fasciculata (Michx.) Greene

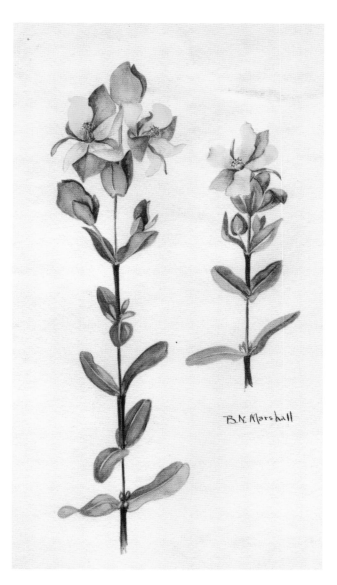

ST. PETER'S-WORT
Hypericum crux-andreae (L.) Crantz

BUSH-CLOVER
Probably *Lespedeza repens* (L.) W. Bart.

FLOWERING SPURGE
Euphorbia corollata L.

PENCIL-FLOWER
Stylosanthes biflora (L.) B.S.P.

B. N. Marshall

STAR-GRASS
Hypoxis hirsuta (L.) Coville

(facing page)

BLUETS

Houstonia caerulea L.

Also known as Quaker ladies, these prim little wildflowers, barely half an inch in diameter, were among the first species planted in the Lee Park sanctuary in the spring of 1936. Sixty years later, small patches bloom in spring in the park's open upland. The yellow-eyed flowers range from white or pale lilac to this serene blue. The seeds germinate in the fall and form a rosette of basal leaves that persists through the winter.

BLUE-EYED GRASS
Sisyrinchium mucronatum Michx.

Spurred Butterfly-Pea
Centrosema virginianum
(L.) Benth.

This vine has upside-down flowers: the broad banner petal points downward, while the smaller keel petals point upward—the opposite of the typical pea flower. This species blooms in summer and early fall on a sunny barren near the old bathhouse at Willcox Lake. Growing nearby is *Clitoria mariana,* a species that also has upside-down flowers and is also called butterfly-pea—which may explain why this painting was incorrectly paired with a specimen of *C. mariana* in the herbarium collection.

B.N. Marshall

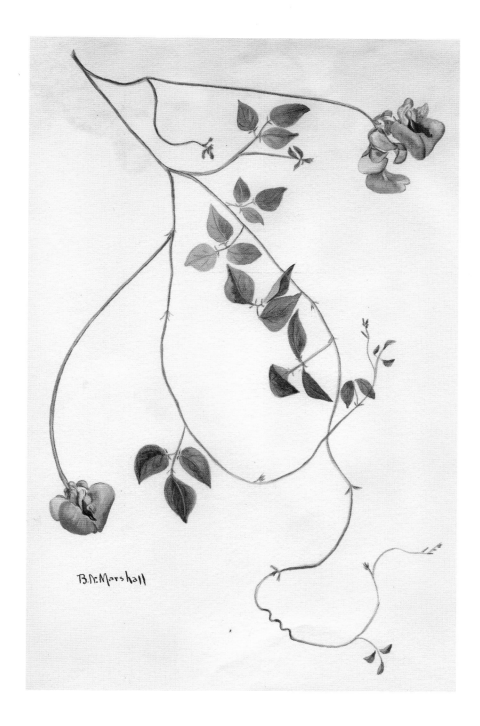

PINK WILD BEAN
Strophostyles umbellata (Muhl. ex Willd.) Britt.

Bessie Marshall's spare composition captures the undulating nature of this petite, perennial climbing vine. The artist chose an unorthodox viewpoint with the plant pointing downward. Usually the dark purple keel petal protrudes like a beak from the *bottom* of the flower, rather than the top, as it does here. The seeds of this plant are woolly.

PINEWEED

Hypericum gentianoides
(L.) B.S.P.

POKEWEED

Phytolacca americana L.

Bessie Marshall put time and thought into her illustration of this some-times irksome weed, which can grow as tall as a small tree. Here she emphasizes both the tops and the undersides of the leaves and lends di-mension to her composition by including leaves in different planes. The juicy berries provided a dye for the Indians and early settlers. When properly cooked, with several rinses in the process, the young shoots and young leaves make a fine "poke salad," but the stems and roots are poisonous.

B. N. Marshall—

(facing page)

WILD FIELD-PANSY

Viola bicolor Pursh

The only native North American pansy, this species grows in dense patches. Although the leaves appear to be compound, they are actually simple leaves with fringed stipules at the nodes where they join the stem. The flowers may vary in color from creamy yellow to deep blue. On the left, Bessie Marshall has highlighted a single plant with pale blue flowers.

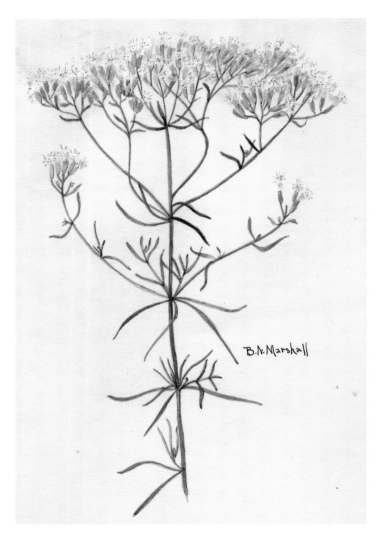

HYSSOP-LEAVED THOROUGHWORT

Eupatorium hyssopifolium L.

B.N.Marshall —

B.N. Marshall

ST. ANDREW'S CROSS
Hypericum hypericoides
(L.) Crantz

B.N.Marshall

INDIAN HEMP

Apocynum cannabinum L.

Each pert little flower of this plant has a pair of ovaries, and each ovary develops into a long, skinny seedpod filled with hair-tufted seeds. The pods yield a milky latex. The outer layer of the red-hued stems contains a hemplike fiber, which the Indians of colonial Virginia dried, then beat into silklike strands that they dyed and wove into baskets.

Low- *or* Pasture-Rose
Rosa carolina L.

This shrub grows knee-high on the slopes of the Civil War breastworks and elsewhere in Lee Park. Bessie Marshall's illustration shows a "thumbprint" depression in one of the petals and the small yellow button—actually the compressed style tips—in the center of the flower. Also depicted are a bud, the straight slender prickles, and a bright red rose hip, rich in vitamin C.

SILK-TREE
Albizia julibrissin Durz.

Introduced to America from tropical Asia, this small tree, also called mimosa, quickly gained admirers and eventually became naturalized. The silky pink "pom-poms" consist of up to two dozen small flowers, each with numerous stamens. The threadlike filaments of the stamens form the tassels of the pom-pom. The fernlike leaflets close up at night.

Passion-Flower

Passiflora incarnata L.

The flamboyant flower of this native vine features a double or triple circle of fringes, and horns on the tips of its green sepals. An elaborate legend draws symbolic parallels between the parts of this flower and the story of the Passion, in which the five anthers signify the five wounds of Christ, the three-branched style stands for the three nails by which Christ was hung from the cross, and the circles of fringes represent the crown of thorns. The plants bear edible fruits, sometimes called maypops, that pop when stomped on.

B.N. Marshall

TRUMPET-CREEPER
Campsis radicans (L.) Seem.
ex Bureau

Masses of trumpet-creeper, a native vine with spectacular trumpet-shaped flowers, festoon the loblolly pines that flank the picnic pavilion at Lee Park. The workers in the WPA sanctuary planted this species on bare spots to hold leaf mulch on the transplanted flowers.

WILD CARROT

Daucus carota L.

This old-world weed, familiarly known as Queen Anne's lace, is probably the ancestor of the garden carrot. Its white, spindle-shaped roots are rich in carotene but disagreeable in flavor. The "flower" of this summer-blooming species is actually a system of flower clusters, each composed of tiny white florets. Some individual plants, such as the one shown here, have one dark purple floret in the middle of the cluster.

B.N. Marshall

CORALBERRY
Symphoricarpos orbiculatus Moench

Common Mullein
Verbascum thapsus L.

Reaching heights of five feet or more, mullein plants rise up like hoary candlesticks along the southern border of Lee Park in June. By mixing watercolor and gouache, Bessie Marshall depicted the velvety texture of the leaves, which are woolly throughout. A naturalized species from Europe, mullein once served as lamp wick, foot warmer, and tobacco substitute. The children of Lee Park worker Lillian Anderson remembered their mother using mullein leaves to bring down a fever and make a tea.

SELF-HEAL *or* HEAL-ALL
Prunella vulgaris L.

COMMON DAY-FLOWER
Commelina communis L.

YELLOW WOOD-SORREL *(top)*
Oxalis dillenii Jacq.

VIOLET WOOD-SORREL *(bottom)*
Oxalis violacea L.

Yellow wood-sorrel occurs in open upland, while violet wood-sorrel grows in forested upland.

GLAUCOUS-LEAVED GREENBRIER
Smilax glauca Walt.

Although common in the woodlands of Lee Park, this vine does not flower in habitats where it is repressed by shade. But in certain open areas of the park, it grows abundantly and flowers profusely. The newest leaves are red; as they mature they turn green. Bessie Marshall's composition ably renders the glaucousness on the undersides of the leaves and also shows a stem in the fruiting stage.

B. N. Marshall

DEWBERRY
Rubus flagellaris Willd.

(facing page)

BLACKBERRY

Rubus bifrons Vest ex Tratt.

Bessie Marshall has illustrated two different stages of this bramble: a prickly branch topped with buds and pale pink flowers, and a branch bearing glistening fruit in various stages, from yellow adolescence to black ripeness. The berries are made up of many small drupelets, each of which contains a single seed inside a bony layer, like a miniature peach pit. As shown here, the veins on the undersides of the leaves are prominent.

DEWBERRY
Rubus flagellaris Willd.
(blunt-leaved variant)

BULBOUS BUTTERCUP

Ranunculus bulbosus L.

DAY-LILY

Hemerocallis fulva (L.) L.

An introduced species from Eurasia, this day-lily was a popular cultivar in colonial times. It persists along roadsides and at old homesites and reproduces from rhizomes. Each flower lasts only one day, but each tall stem bears many flowers. The edges of the three inner tepals pucker as shown here.

DEPTFORD-PINK
Dianthus armeria L.

The delightful pink flowers of
this introduced European
species are freckled with white.
The petals have jagged outer
edges, as if cut with pinking
shears, which is how this species
and its relatives came to be
called "pinks." Later the word
"pink" also came to mean the
light rose color found in many
such flowers. Like other members of the carnation family,
the Deptford-pink has swollen
nodes where the leaves join the
stem.

B. N. Marshall

Forested Upland

Forests still cover much of Lee Park. On the slopes above Willcox Lake, which have not been harvested for timber for many years, one finds maturing forests of mixed hardwoods, including northern red oak, scarlet oak, American beech, and chestnut oak with its distinctively fissured bark. The steep angle of these slopes permits enough light to reach the forest floor to support dense patches of huckleberry, mountain laurel, and other species. On the more protected slopes, white oak finds a home.

On the plateau above these slopes, some of the woodlands have been selectively cut, producing a younger forest that includes southern red oak, white oak, various hickories, and black gum, interspersed with loblolly pine and shortleaf pine. Sufficient light passes through the gaps in the canopy for blueberries and huckleberries to persist in bushy stands. Some interior sections of the plateau, as well as some of the gentler slopes, have been clear-cut and have regrown into a thicket of tulip-tree, with some sweet gum and red maple intermingled. Along the Civil War breastworks, a broad band of maturing loblolly pine has been spared from clear-cutting.

In the 1930s, pine dominated the southern section of the forested upland, but only a few pine stands remain—a consequence of timbering and forest succession. This area harbors pink lady's-slipper, large whorled pogonia, and many other species that Bessie Marshall painted.

HIGHBUSH BLUEBERRY
probably *Vaccinium formosum* Andr.
(black-fruited variant)

VARIOUS BERRY BUSHES

Depicted here are four—or possibly five—species in flower and in fruit.
The dangleberry, *Gaylussacia frondosa* (L.) Torr. & Gray ex Torr. (top), bears
glaucous blue fruit that is tasty but gritty. The branches in the center are
ambiguous. The flowering stem may be the black highbush blueberry
(*Vaccinium fuscatum* Ait.), but the fruiting stem is probably the highbush
blueberry (*Vaccinium formosum* Andr.); or both may be New Jersey blueberry (*Vaccinium caesariense* Mackenzie). The dwarf early blueberry, *Vaccinium pallidum* Ait. (lower right), has very sweet berries. The dwarf
huckleberry, *Gaylussacia dumosa* (Andr.) Torr. & Gray (lower left), has
lustrous leaves and shiny black fruit.

(facing page)

DEERBERRY

Vaccinium stamineum L.

Distinguished from other blueberries in Lee Park by its protruding stamens and bell-shaped flowers, the deerberry was mentioned in the plant catalogue developed in the seventeenth century by Virginia naturalist John Banister. This shrub is common in the upland woods of Lee Park. Bessie Marshall ably portrayed the glaucousness on the berries and the undersides of the leaves.

BLACK HUCKLEBERRY

Gaylussacia baccata (Wangenh.) K. Koch

SMALL BLACK BLUEBERRY

Vaccinium tenellum Ait.

B. N. Marshall

Strawberry-Bush

Euonymus americanus L.

The twig at the top displays the green stems, finely toothed leaves, and subtly colored flowers of this leggy shrub. But perhaps the most interesting feature is the crimson fruit capsule dotted with warts. As shown here, these capsules burst open to expose five seeds with fleshy, scarlet-orange coats— which explains why this plant is also called hearts-a-bustin'. A faint pencil sketch of another twig is visible above the capsule; why Bessie Marshall never finished painting it is a mystery.

B. M. Marshall

STAGGERBUSH
Lyonia mariana (L.) D. Don

DWARF THORN
Crataegus uniflora Muenchh.

HAZEL-NUT

Corylus americana Walt.

Here Bessie Marshall combines three different elements of this shrub in a polished arrangement with contrast, depth, and skillfully rendered detail. The grayish brown catkins, which form on the branches in the fall, are strands of small male flowers that release their pollen in early spring. The ovaries of the female flowers (not shown here) mature into delicious nuts. Each nut sits inside a helmetlike husk ("corylus" is Greek for helmet) with a sharply lacerated, ruffled edge.

B. N. Marshall

WITCH-HAZEL

Hamamelis virginiana L.

This shrub, which blooms in
October in Lee Park, has four
yellow petals that resemble
straggly straps. After the petals
drop, the four burgundy sepals
persist. The Indians of Virginia
used a distillate of witch-hazel
bark to treat muscular aches and
various illnesses. Eighteenth-
century botanist John Clayton
sent artist Mark Catesby a gift of
a Virginia witch-hazel shrub; it
arrived from its transatlantic
voyage in bloom for Christmas.

(facing page)

TRAILING ARBUTUS
Epigaea repens L.

In early March, the pink-to-white flowers of this creeping species emerge along the steep slopes of Lee Park, emitting a wonderfully spicy fragrance. The evergreen leaves are rather leathery and sometimes mottled, as shown here. Colonial botanist John Banister sketched this species, and Bessie Marshall liked her own watercolor well enough to send it to a prospective client in Richmond.

WILD HYDRANGEA
Hydrangea arborescens L.

B.N.Marshall

B.N.Marshall

NEW JERSEY TEA
Ceanothus americanus L.

Mountain Laurel
Kalmia latifolia L.

"A high hill and a shrub" was the clue for the mountain laurel in the memory game devised by the WPA supervisors of the Lee Park sanctuary. Although more commonly associated with the mountains, this species also thrives in the coastal plain, especially on steep, north-facing slopes. Bessie Marshall added a realistic touch to this painting by showing splotches on one of the leaves. The leaves remain green through the winter.

PIPSISSEWA *or* PRINCE'S PINE
Chimaphila umbellata (L.) W. Bart.

(facing page)
RATTLESNAKE-MASTER
Eryngium yuccifolium Michx.

Rattlesnake-master, which is rare in Virginia north of the James River, was included in the 1739 *Flora Virginica* compiled by colonial botanist John Clayton. Dr. James Greenway, another early botanist who lived near Petersburg, considered this species an excellent remedy for rattlesnake bite. The flower heads consist of greenish florets mingled with bractlets that resemble miniature artichoke bracts; with age they assume the purplish cast shown here.

SPOTTED WINTERGREEN
Chimaphila maculata (L.) Pursh

B.N.Marshall

Virginia Wild Ginger
Hexastylis virginica (L.) Small

The little brown jugs, as the flowers of this plant are often called, consist of sepals but no petals. They often lie hidden beneath leaf litter and are pollinated by crawling insects. Later, ants disseminate the mature seeds by carrying them to their nests. Although this species is not related to commercial ginger, its peppery rhizomes are sometimes candied. John Banister, one of the first naturalists in Virginia, made a drawing of this species that was acquired by the British Museum.

INDIAN CUCUMBER-ROOT
Medeola virginiana L.

Young plants of Indian cucumber-root send up a stem with a whorl of leaves. As the plant matures, it produces a second-story whorl. From this upper whorl emerges a small umbel of nodding, yellow-green flowers with red styles and red anthers. As shown here, the wiry stem has cottony patches of flocculus that can be rubbed off. (This is one way to tell the Indian cucumber-root from smooth-stemmed whorled pogonias.) The rhizome of this species tastes a bit like cucumber.

RUE-ANEMONE

Thalictrum thalictroides (L.)
Eames & Boiv.

This early spring bloomer is
characterized by clusters of
tubers, shown to full effect in
Bessie Marshall's arching composition. The finely veined sepals
(it has no petals) vary in color
from white to the pinkish form
depicted on the right.

B.N.Marshall

WILD COLUMBINE
Aquilegia canadensis L.

John Tradescant the Younger, who botanized along the James and York Rivers in 1637, took seeds of wild columbine to England, and soon it became a prized addition to Europe's finest gardens. The wild columbine has a nodding flower: the sepals point downward and the five long petals project upwards into spurs—the horns of the cuckold in the lore of flowers. The spurs hold nectar that hummingbirds extract with their long tongues.

WHORLED ROSIN-WEED
Silphium trifoliatum L.

Bessie Marshall painted two different sections of this very tall plant. The small, five-lobed flowers of the central disk are sterile, while the straplike ray flowers are fertile—the opposite of the sunflower, which has sterile ray flowers and fertile disk flowers (the source of sunflower "seeds"). Also shown are several flower heads in bud or just beginning to expand, along with one green, rosette-shaped head that has finished flowering.

GREAT *or* STAR CHICKWEED *(top)*
Stellaria pubera Michx.

COMMON CHICKWEED *(lower left)*
Stellaria media (L.) Vill.

MOUSE-EAR CHICKWEED *(lower right)*
Cerastium glomeratum Thuill.

Great Chickweed grows in forested upland; the other two chickweeds in this illustration grow in open upland.

BLOODROOT
Sanguinaria canadensis L.

PENNYWORT
Obolaria virginica L.

Barely six inches tall, this
compact plant would have been
difficult to spot as it poked
through the leaf litter in the
moist woodlands of Lee Park
in the 1930s. Normally the
whitish section of the lower
stem, shown here, would be
concealed beneath leaf litter. The
faintly purple to white flowers
emerge early in the spring. The
penny-shaped leaves become
mottled with age. (The genus
name comes from the Greek
"obolus," or small coin.)

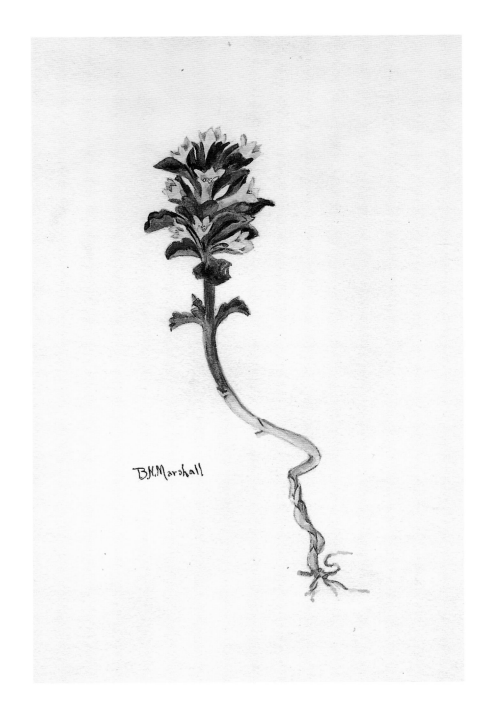

EVERLASTING *or* PUSSYTOES
Antennaria solitaria Rydb.

ROBIN'S PLANTAIN
Erigeron pulchellus Michx.

EARLY SAXIFRAGE
Saxifraga virginiensis Michx.

(facing page)

GALAX

Galax urceolata (Poir.) Brummitt

Galax can be recognized by its wand of tiny milk-white flowers and its rounded leaves with a heart-shaped base. The leaves, which are green in summer, turn reddish in autumn. Galax still grows in acidic soils on the steep ravine slopes of Lee Park. In keeping with the style of many classical botanical illustrators, Bessie Marshall depicted the root system.

HEPATICA *or* LIVER LEAF
Hepatica americana (DC.) Ker-Gawl.

HAIRY MEADOW-PARSNIP
Thaspium barbinode (Michx.) Nutt.

(facing page)
WHITE MILKWEED
Asclepias variegata L.

The white globes of this species are actually crowded umbels of small white flowers with deep purple centers. Bessie Marshall's painting also features several unopened buds and an inset of a single flower, with its elevated crown. In several blossoms, the artist used the off-white background of the paper to represent the white of the crowns. As shown here, the cut stem yields a milky juice.

HAIRY ANGELICA
Angelica venenosa (Greenway) Fern.

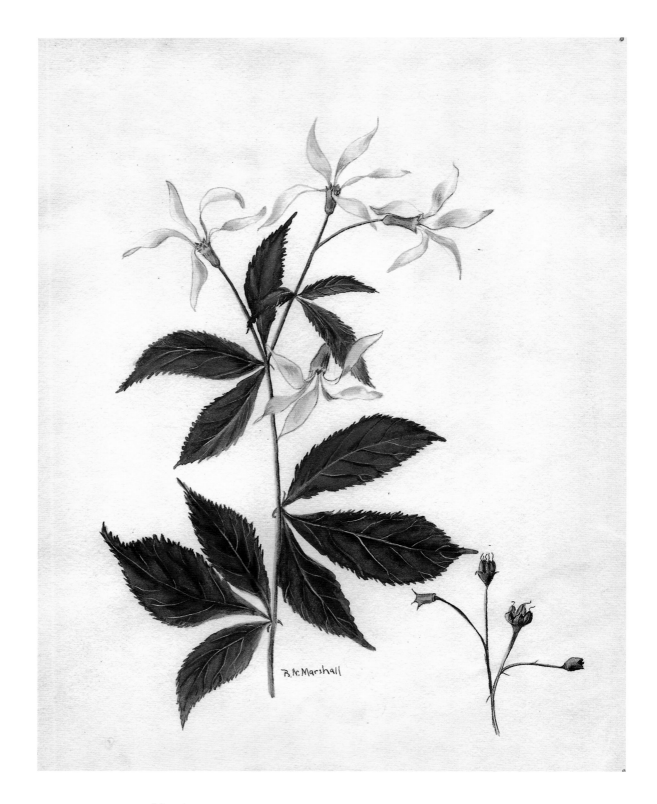

B. M. Marshall

SMALL-LEAVED WHITE SNAKEROOT
Ageratina aromatica (L.) Spach

INDIAN-PHYSIC *or* FALSE IPECAC
Porteranthus trifoliatus (L.) Britt.

When these stark-white flowers bloom in June,
they make an attractive contrast with the rich green
leaves. The inset shows the follicles of the fruit in
various stages of maturation. William Byrd II, a
colonial leader who lived near Petersburg, swore
by this species as a remedy for the "flux."

Adam and Eve
or Putty-Root
Aplectrum hyemale (Muhl.
ex Willd.) Torr.

The "Adam" and "Eve" of this orchid are the two joined bulbs—actually corms—that resemble giant garlic cloves. When bruised, the corms yield a glutinous putty, adhesive enough to mend china. The large pleated leaf (center), striped with white veins, comes up in autumn and lasts through winter. In late spring a flowering stem (left) emerges and blooms, while the leaf dies back. The stem remains standing (right) as the fruit capsules mature.

B.N.Marshall

Showy Orchis

Galearis spectabilis (L.) Raf.

Finding a showy orchis is a rare delight for orchid aficionados, who often have a special fondness for its appealing color combination, fleshy leaves, and graceful but substantial flowers. Two petals and three sepals comprise the lavender hood. The white lower lip has a long spur filled with sweet syrup. This succulent-leaved species grows in humus over nutrient-rich soils, which are uncommon in Lee Park.

SMALL WHORLED POGONIA
Isotria medeoloides (Pursh) Raf.

In 1982 the small whorled pogonia was placed on the federally endangered list, and it remains rare throughout most of its range. None of these three illustrations quite captures the intriguing demeanor of this small orchid; perhaps Bessie Marshall painted them from pressed specimens. At first the leaves clasp tightly around the bud, but as the flower develops, they separate. Eventually the whorl of leaves droops, and the sepals spread apart. When the flowers are mature, the leaves usually rise to a horizontal position.

B.N.Marshall

Large Whorled Pogonia
Isotria verticillata Raf.

More common than the small whorled pogonia, this orchid occurs in the older pine woods and on the hardwood slopes of Lee Park. This painting shows a budding flower (center), a partially opened flower (left), and a mature flower with three radically elongated sepals (right). As the flower opens, a whorl of leaves unfurls beneath it. In the mature flower, the top two petals form a green hood over the white lip petal, and the multicolored sepals extend to two or three times the length of the petals.

CRANE-FLY ORCHIS
Tipularia discolor (Pursh) Nutt.

RATTLESNAKE-PLANTAIN
Goodyera pubescens (Willd.) R. Br. ex Ait. f.

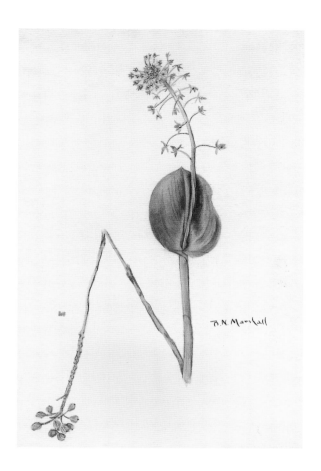

GREEN ADDER'S-MOUTH
Malaxis unifolia Michx.

PINK LADY'S-SLIPPER
or STEMLESS LADY'S-SLIPPER
Cypripedium acaule Ait.

Hoary Mountain-Mint

Pycnanthemum incanum (L.) Michx.

The colors of this species are subtle, but its fragrance is strongly minty. The small flowers (see inset) are a soft white or lavender, with purple spots. They grow in dense clusters, which accounts for the botanical name ("pychos" means dense and "anthemon" means flower). The leaf color shifts gradually from almost white at the base to green near the tip. Fine hairs lend a grayish-white cast to the upper leaves and bracts and the undersides of the lower leaves.

B. W. Marshall

DOWNY PHLOX
Phlox pilosa L.

BLUE-HEARTS
Buchnera americana L.

WHORLED TICKSEED *or* COREOPSIS
Coreopsis verticillata L.

WILD *or* YELLOW INDIGO
Baptisia tinctoria (L.) R. Br. ex Ait. f.

RATTLESNAKE-WEED
Hieracium venosum L.

BASTARD TOAD-FLAX
Comandra umbellata (L.) Nutt.

GOLDEN-KNEE *or* GREEN-AND-GOLD
Chrysogonum virginianum L.

DOWNY FALSE FOXGLOVE
Aureolaria virginica (L.) Pennell

B.K.Marshall

FERN-LEAVED FALSE FOXGLOVE

Aureolaria pedicularia (L.) Raf.

This annual false foxglove may grow to more than three feet tall in Lee Park. It is "hemiparasitic": although it photosynthesizes, it is also a parasite on tree roots. Bessie Marshall used two stalks to create this pleasantly busy composition of ragged leaves, funnel-shaped flowers, and threadlike styles, which become obvious once the corolla has fallen away.

B. N. Marshall

WILD LUPINE

Lupinus perennis L.

(facing page)

CAROLINA-LILY

Lilium michauxii Poir.

Bessie Marshall's three views highlight several captivating features of this splendid plant: the strongly recurved tepals, the extravagantly protruding filaments, and the scarlet anthers, which seem almost to rock back and forth on their fulcrums. She also captures the sumptuous blend of colors in the flowers. The leaves of this species widen near the top—one way to distinguish it from the turk's-cap lily. Petersburg is very near the northern limit of the entire range of this lily.

WHORLED LOOSESTRIFE

Lysimachia quadrifolia L.

TRUMPET-HONEYSUCKLE
Lonicera sempervirens L.

This native honeysuckle—a
favorite of hummingbirds—is
actually a shrub with a woody
stem from which new green
twining stems emerge. The
fragrant, trumpet-shaped
flowers are yellow inside and
red outside; at the base of the
flower tube sits the glaucous
green ovary. On the left is a
close-up of the soft, almost
translucent red berries. The
uppermost leaves, which are
evergreen in southeastern
Virginia, fuse at the stem.

PERIWINKLE
Vinca minor L.

This trailing native of Europe often forms a solid ground cover in shady spots. In the forested hinterlands, a patch of periwinkle signals that an old home probably once stood nearby, even if no other vestiges remain. This illustration shows the glossy leaves and the white, star-shaped outline in the center of the pinwheel-like purple flowers.

HAIRY WOOD SUNFLOWER
or PURPLE-DISK SUNFLOWER
Helianthus atrorubens L.

SERVICEBERRY *or* SHADBUSH
Amelanchier canadensis (L.) Medik.

CAROLINA *or* PALE VETCH
Vicia caroliniana Walt.

HAWTHORN

Crataegus flabellata (Spach) Kirchn.

The thorns of this shrub thrust out ominously in all directions, as if to keep intruders away from the exquisite white flowers. The fan-shaped leaves of the flowering branches are a noteworthy characteristic. In September, the hawthorn bears applelike fruits, maroon in color, that can be cooked down to make jelly.

B.N. Marshall

Chinquapin

Castanea pumila (L.) P. Mill.

This native shrub or small tree is common on the slopes above Willcox Lake. Ensconced within each spiny green bur is a single nutritious nut, which the coastal plain Indians enjoyed and which people still seek out for its sweet flavor. Above the burs are remnants of staminate flowers. The leaves have coarse teeth and a hairy grayish felt on their undersides.

PERSIMMON
Diospyros virginiana L.

This spare but arresting illustration of the persimmon tree highlights its glaucous fruits. The rusty-orange ripe fruits have a pleasant taste and served as food to the American Indians, but when green, the fruit has a mouth-pursing astringency. A single persimmon tree produces small yellowish flowers that are either male or female.

Redbud *or* Judas Tree
Cercis canadensis L.

The flower clusters of this deciduous tree are fastened directly onto the mature branches. In the 1930s, WPA workers planted hundreds of redbuds in Lee Park, donated as memorials by local citizens. Only a few have survived; the soils are probably too acidic for this species. Its common name derives from the story that Judas Iscariot hanged himself from a Eurasian species of *Cercis*.

TULIP-TREE
Liriodendron tulipifera L.

FLOWERING DOGWOOD

Cornus florida L.

Among the several species of dogwood native to Virginia, this is the only one with large white "petals"
(actually modified leaves); the other species have just
the central cluster of small yellow flowers. Each yellow flower cluster becomes a cluster of red fruits,
also shown here.

B.N.Marshall

B.K. Marshall

SQUAREHEAD
Tetragonotheca helianthoides L.

SILKY LEATHER-FLOWER
Clematis ochroleuca Ait.

(facing page)
AMERICAN HOLLY
Ilex opaca Ait.

Individual holly trees bear either female flowers or male flowers. This tree had female flowers, but at the stage shown here, the ovaries have ripened into opaque, red fruits. The mottling on the leaves may be mildew. Charles Gillette, a Richmond landscape architect who helped to design the Norfolk WPA wildflower sanctuary in the 1930s, proposed the holly as the official emblem of Richmond.

HAIRY RUELLIA *or* WILD-PETUNIA
Ruellia caroliniensis (J. F. Gmel.) Steud.

LARGE HOUSTONIA
Houstonia purpurea L.

WILD YAM
Dioscorea villosa L.

WILD BLACK CHERRY
Prunus serotina Ehrh.

Sessile-Leaved Bellwort
Uvularia sessilifolia L.

Yellow Colic-Root
Aletris aurea Walt.

EBONY-SPLEENWORT
Asplenium platyneuron (L.) B.S.P.

ROCK POLYPODY
Polypodium virginianum L.

PARTRIDGE-BERRY
Mitchella repens L.

PARTRIDGE-BERRY
Mitchella repens L.

Open Bottomland

The open lowland habitats of Lee Park range from moist to wet and from very sunny to partly shaded. The narrow margins of open land surrounding Willcox Lake form an extensive sunny habitat for moisture-loving species like buttonbush and alder. In the 1930s, there was a significant boggy habitat at the mouth of a ravine on the western edge of the lake. (This area was just upstream of a small circular inlet, visible in the map on page 94, on the west side of Willcox Lake, north of the loop road and south of the Civil War breastworks.) In a wide sphagnous ravine bottom, called the "bog" by the WPA supervisors, the WPA workers planted pitcher-plants, rare orchids, and other bog-loving species. Since the 1930s, the lake has risen about ten feet, and most of the bog is now under water.

At the head of the lake, in the southern section of Lee Park, the bottomland is choked with invasive rice-cut-grass and arrow-leaved tearthumb, but one can still find spotted touch-me-not and cat-tail. Just upstream, beavers have dammed the flow of Willcox Branch, creating a pond. Some of this area may have been a natural swamp in the 1930s, but even then the beavers were at work. Further upstream, near the park road crossing, stands of alder and river birch fringe an open pond.

A portion of the power-line cut lies in the floodplain of Willcox Branch, forming another open bottomland habitat for joe-pye weed, meadow-beauty, and common elder.

A forest fire in the 1930s created a section of open bottomland in the floodplain of Willcox Branch, north of the lake. Although the area has been reforested, the Japanese honeysuckle planted there to stabilize the soil still remains.

SPOTTED TOUCH-ME-NOT
Impatiens capensis Meerb.

The splotched orange flowers of this species dangle like jewels from the stalks (another common name is jewel-weed). The striking flower has a long spur that curves forward from a rotund sac formed by one of the three sepals. Hikers exposed to poison ivy or stinging nettles can sometimes prevent a rash or quell the sting by rubbing their skin with crushed stems of this species, which often grows alongside. At the slightest touch, the ripened seed capsules will explode, sending seeds flying everywhere.

B.N.Marshall

PICKEREL-WEED
Pontederia cordata L.

This aquatic herb sometimes shares quiet lake edges with pickerel fish. This illustration portrays the swooping pattern of parallel veins in the long heart-shaped leaves. As shown here, the upper middle tepal of the six-part flower has two tiny yellow spots that resemble eyes.

COMMON CAT-TAIL
Typha latifolia L.

Bessie Marshall's diagonal composition of the cat-tail shows the pollen-producing spike of flowers at the top and the pebbled, brown, seed-producing cob below. In colonial times the cat-tail, which still grows in the marshy lowlands of Lee Park, was valued for its sweet pod, according to botanist John Clayton's 1739 description in *Flora Virginica*.

BUTTONBUSH
Cephalanthus occidentalis L.

This water-loving shrub grows along the margins of Willcox Lake. Small white tubular flowers with protruding styles form a large perfect sphere, about an inch and a half in diameter. The two lower flower heads are in the bud stage.

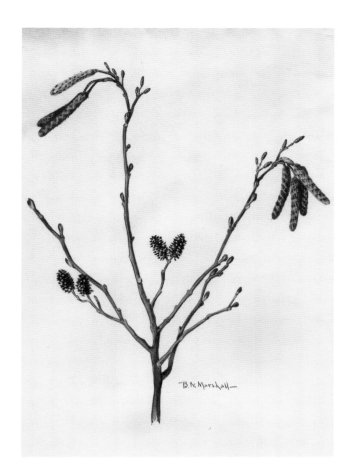

SMOOTH ALDER
Alnus serrulata (Ait.) Willd.

COMMON ELDER
Sambucus canadensis L.

Arrow-Arum
Peltandra virginica (L.) Schott

Male flowers cover the exposed rod of the spadix of this aquatic species, which has arrow-shaped leaves. The cluster of developing fruits on the lower part of the spadix causes the spathe to bulge, as shown. As the spathes rot in the mud, they release mucilaginous marble-sized fruits—unappealing to humans but a favorite of wood ducks. American Indians sometimes made bread from the tuberous root, which had a virulent taste when raw.

BROAD-LEAVED ARROW-HEAD
Sagittaria latifolia Willd.

Stalks of this aquatic species rise up from a base of large leaves, which are shaped like arrowheads. Beneath the mud, the fibrous roots produce edible tubers, called swamp potatoes or duck potatoes. Both the flowers and the fruit heads occur in whorls of three. The small green fruit heads, shown clinging to the stalk below the flowers, hold hundreds of minute winged fruits.

BLUE FLAG

Iris virginica L.

This majestic wild iris grows in
one cove along Willcox Lake.
The six-part flower features
hairy yellow markings along the
sepals, which may help to guide
pollinating insects. This illustration highlights the attractive vein
patterns of the lavender-blue
flowers.

SLENDER BLUE FLAG

Iris prismatica Pursh ex Ker-Gawl.

This comely blue flag is on the Virginia Heritage Watchlist, a list of species uncommon in Virginia that should be protected. Primarily a coastal species, it grows along shorelines, in brackish and freshwater marshes, and in meadows. It has much narrower leaves than the southern blue flag (*I. virginica*).

B.N. Marshall

Bunch-Flower

Melanthium virginicum L.

This rather tall plant likes wet habitats but rarely occurs in the coastal plain. Its cream-colored flowers, highlighted here against a backdrop of dark green leaves, take on green and purple tinges as they age. The flowers consist of six tepals, each with two small green glands at the base, shown here.

JOE-PYE WEED
Eupatorium fistulosum Barratt

P ENNSYLVANIA K NOTWEED
Polygonum pensylvanicum L.

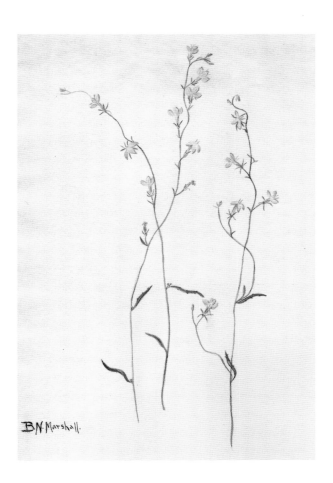

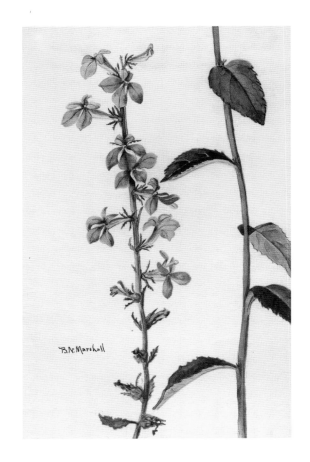

GREAT LOBELIA
Lobelia siphilitica L.

White Fringed Orchis

Platanthera blephariglottis
(Willd.) Lindl. var. *conspicua*
(Nash) Luer

Recorded in only nine counties in Virginia, this very rare species features a large cluster of pure white flowers on a tall sturdy stem. The species name comes from "blephar," which means eyelid, and "glottis," which means tongue—so called because the fringe around the single lip petal looks like a tongue decorated with eyelashes. Giant stands of white fringed orchis once flourished in southeastern Virginia.

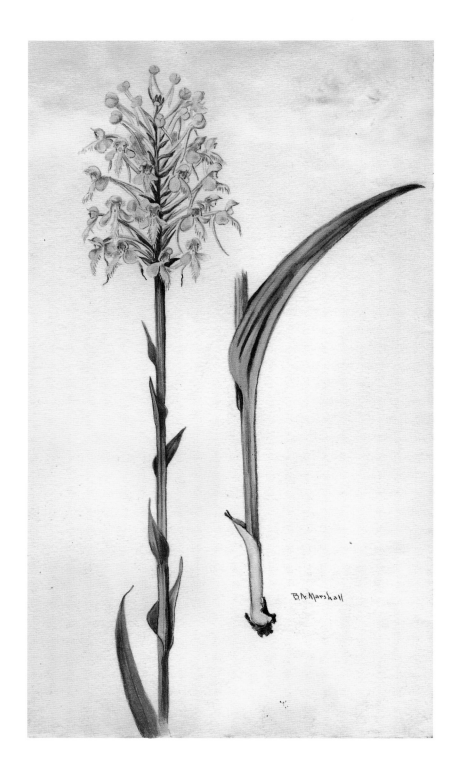

B.A.Marshall

YELLOW FRINGED ORCHIS
Platanthera ciliaris (L.) Lindl.

LINEAR-LEAVED LADIES' TRESSES
Spiranthes vernalis Engelm. & Gray

ROSE POGONIA
Pogonia ophioglossoides (L.) Ker-Gawl.

SPREADING POGONIA
Cleistes divaricata (L.) Ames

B.N.Marshall

GRASS-PINK
Calopogon tuberosus (L.)
B.S.P.

The WPA workers trans-
planted this rare and fancy
orchid with grasslike leaves
into the sanctuary's sphagnum bog. The grass-pink has
an "upside-down" flower,
with the yellow-bearded lip
on top. (Most orchids start
out with the lip on top, but
twist a half-turn as the
flower bud develops.) The
bearded lip has a weak
"hinge" near the base. When
an insect alights, the lip
petal gives way, and the insect drops down to the col-
umn where the stigma and
pollen await.

B. N. Marshall

PITCHER-PLANT

Sarracenia purpurea L.

This carnivorous bog dweller seemed so strange to
the colonial botanist John Banister that he described
the plant as "monstrous" and almost unreal. The plant
has inflated leaves, the pitchers, that collect water.
Hapless insects slip into the water, drown, and are
digested. (Note the tiny insect on one leaf.) This
species, now very rare in Virginia, has a huge style
that thrusts forward like an umbrella.

HAIRY PIPEWORT

Lachnocaulon anceps (Walt.) Morong

RED MILKWEED
Asclepias rubra L.

HAIRY SWAMP-MILKWEED
Asclepias incarnata L. ssp. *pulchra*
(Ehrh. ex Willd.) Woods.

ORANGE MILKWORT
Polygala lutea L.

FALSE ASPHODEL
Tofieldia racemosa (Walt.) B.S.P.

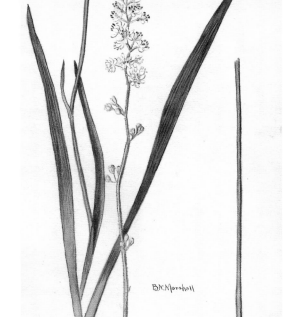

B.N.Marshall

TRUMPETS
Sarracenia flava L.

Trumpets once flourished in Dinwiddie County, Virginia, their northern limit. The hooded pitchers, with their prominent red veins, may stand more than two feet tall. The plant absorbs nitrogen and other nutrients not found in boggy habitats from insects that die inside the pitchers. Today the species is critically imperiled in Virginia.

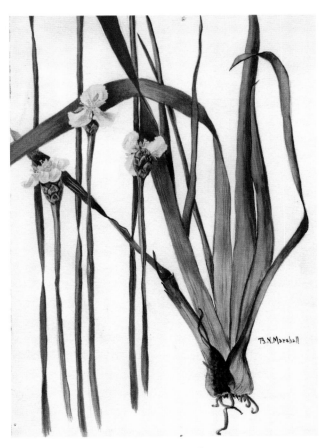

YELLOW-EYED GRASS
Probably *Xyris difformis* Chapman var. *difformis*

MARYLAND MEADOW-BEAUTY
Rhexia mariana L. var. *mariana*

NARROW-LEAVED SUNFLOWER
Helianthus angustifolius L.

Forested Bottomland

Forested bottomland habitats in Lee Park have dwindled considerably since the 1930s. A wooded swamp that once existed in the southern section has been flooded, a victim of beaver dams and clogs of debris in the culvert under the park road. Bottomland that was once forested is now open or inhabited by thickets of alder.

One large remaining area of forested floodplain lies along a tributary of Willcox Branch near the head of the lake. Beneath the canopy of red maple and other young hardwoods grow yellow-root, stands of cane, and tangles of greenbrier.

The other main habitat of forested floodplain occurs between the dam and its confluence with Lieutenant Run—the same area opened up by a fire in the 1930s. Here the canopy, ragged from timbering, is composed mostly of American elm, sweet gum, red maple, and tulip-tree. Poison ivy, Japanese honeysuckle, and other aggressive or weedy plants proliferate, with some wildflowers intermixed.

The heart of the WPA sanctuary—a series of ravines along the western side of Willcox Lake—is still accessible by trail. Tucked into the upper reaches of one ravine (too small to be shown in the map on page 94) is a sphagnous seep, home to skunk-cabbage, turtlehead, and laurel-magnolia.

SHRUB YELLOW-ROOT
Xanthorhiza simplicissima
Marsh.

Whittling a branch or root of this low shrub reveals a deep yellow color—hence its common name. Thick stands of yellow-root, more typically at home on the banks of mountain streams, grow in the stream head of the tributary that flows into Willcox Lake from the west. What look like petals are actually brownish red sepals.

B.N. Marshall

WINTERBERRY

Ilex verticillata (L.) Gray

WINTERBERRY

Ilex verticillata (L.) Gray

Fringe-Tree

Chionanthus virginicus L.

The fringelike clusters of white flowers droop from the old wood, rather than the new growth, of this small native tree. The fruits, which appear in the fall, resemble blue olives. Eighteenth-century botanist John Clayton grew fringe-trees in his Gloucester County garden, which fellow botanist John Bartram declared to be the most beautiful garden in Virginia.

SPICE-BUSH
Lindera benzoin (L.) Blume

RED CHOKEBERRY
Aronia arbutifolia (L.) Pers.

Sweet Pepper-Bush
Clethra alnifolia L.

Thickets of sweet pepperbush proliferate on the lower wooded slopes just above Willcox Lake. This species is mostly restricted to the coastal plain throughout its range, from Nova Scotia to Texas and Florida. As shown here, the shrub has a sinuous stem, topped with clusters of sweetly scented flowers. The red anthers resemble tiny flecks of red pepper, accounting for its name.

B. K. Marshall

SWAMP-AZALEA
Rhododendron viscosum (L.) Torr.

SWAMP-FETTERBUSH
Leucothoe racemosa (L.) Gray

RAGGED FRINGED ORCHIS
Platanthera lacera (Michx.) G. Don

LARGER YELLOW
LADY'S-SLIPPER
Cypripedium parviflorum
Salisb. var. *pubescens* (Willd.)
Knight

SMALL GREEN WOOD ORCHIS
Platanthera clavellata (Michx.) Luer

B.N. Marshall

TWAYBLADE

Liparis liliifolia (L.) L.C. Rich.
ex Ker-Gawl.

This enchanting species of
orchid was a highlight of the
native wildflower exhibit sponsored by the Virginia Department of Agriculture in 1935. Its
distinctive flower features a wide
lip of diaphanous mauve veined
with purple and two purple
lateral petals as fine as thread.
The three green sepals are larger
but also slender. The name *twayblade* refers to the two leaves.

ATAMASCO-LILY
Zephyranthes atamasca (L.)
Herbert

Also called Jamestown lily,
this species is native to the
coastal plain of the southeastern United States;
Petersburg is near the
northern limit of its entire
range. The snow-white
flowers bloom in spring on
leafless stalks that may
reach a foot or more.

TURK'S-CAP LILY
Lilium superbum L.

Bessie Marshall used layers of wash to achieve the deep oranges of the turk's-cap lily flower and the browns of its dangling anthers and withering blossoms. This painting shows only the upper portion of the plant, which is the largest and most dramatic of the native lilies. The lower half of the stem would include additional whorls of leaves.

Red Maple

Acer rubrum L.

In Lee Park the red maple forms part of the upper canopy in the moist bottomland and part of the lower canopy and understory on the upland. Bessie Marshall must have worked on this painting in multiple sittings, since this tree blooms several weeks before it produces leaves. This species is red in all of its seasonal aspects— petals, winter buds, leaf petioles, and ripe fruits—and in autumn its leaves turn either bright red or yellow. The painstakingly rendered leaf shows the sharp notches between the lobes that distinguish this species from sugar maple.

LAUREL-MAGNOLIA *or* SWEET BAY

Magnolia virginiana L.

The first live magnolia to arrive in Europe was this native Virginia species, sent by botanist John Banister in 1688. This small tree grows in sphagnous stream heads and low woods and produces magnificent, sweet-smelling flowers. Tucked inside the flower is a "cone" of pistils, which eventually ripens into a compound fruit (see inset). The fruit releases its red seeds on silky threads. The slightly leathery evergreen leaves are glaucous on the underside and have a pleasant pungent odor when crushed.

Japanese Honeysuckle
Lonicera japonica Thunb.

Introduced long ago from Asia, this aggressive shrub twines over underbrush and sprawls across open ground, engulfing other species. It has spread to problematic proportions in some areas of Lee Park—most notably on the floodplain below the dam, where the WPA workers planted it to control erosion after a fire, and where timbering has more recently opened the canopy to sunlight. The fragrant flowers start out white, then turn yellow with age. The black berries are enjoyed by birds and mammals.

B. N. Marshall

LAUREL-LEAVED GREENBRIER *or* BAMBOO
Smilax laurifolia L.

TALL *or* GREEN-HEADED CONEFLOWER
Rudbeckia laciniata L.

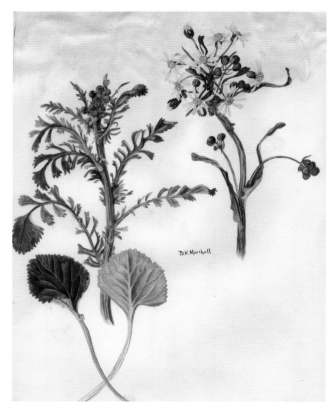

GOLDEN RAGWORT
Senecio aureus L.

TURTLEHEAD
Chelone glabra L.

The WPA workers planted these flowers in the bog of the Lee Park sanctuary during the spring of 1935, and they can still be found near the margins of Willcox Lake. "Chelone" is the Greek word for tortoise, and the flowers are shaped somewhat like a turtle's head. When large bees wiggle around inside the mouth of the flower, it looks as if the plant is chewing.

B. N. Marshall

Dog-Tooth Violet

Erythronium umbilicatum Parks & Hardin

The leaves of this plant—not a violet at all—are mottled like a speckled trout, which is why it is sometimes called trout lily. The bulb, said to resemble a dog's tooth, descends deep into the ground as the plant ages. A seedling is shown on the far left. This species often grows in large colonies of mostly sterile plants (which have just one leaf instead of the two shown here).

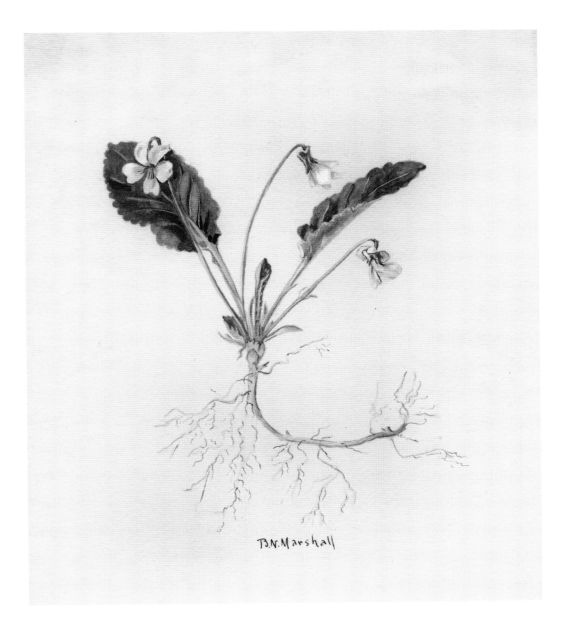

PRIMROSE-LEAVED VIOLET
Viola primulifolia L.

This violet blooms in April and May along the mossy banks of small streams in Lee Park. The three lower petals of its fragrant five-part flower are veined with purple, barely visible here.

Jack-in-the-Pulpit

Arisaema triphyllum (L.) Schott

Found along woodland streams in Lee Park, this species forms male flowers until it can store enough food to generate seed-producing female flowers instead. Later it may revert to producing male flowers. Bessie Marshall has illustrated both the green and the purple genetic forms of the species. She also shows the erect club-like "jack," or spadix, nested inside the hoodlike "pulpit," or spathe. After the spathe withers, the cluster of red berries appears.

Gentian

Gentiana sp.

This watercolor is ambiguous, with characteristics of both soapwort-gentian (*Gentiana saponaria*) and coastal plain gentian (*Gentiana catesbaei*).

Spring-Beauty
Claytonia virginica L.

Carolus Linnaeus honored Gloucester County botanist John Clayton by naming the genus of this native plant after him; today the spring-beauty is the emblem of the John Clayton chapter of the Virginia Native Plant Society. The ephemeral flowers are often white with fine pink pinstripes but can range to a deep pink with darker pinstripes.

Wild Crane's Bill
Geranium maculatum L.

B.N.Marshall —

B.N.Marshall

SKUNK-CABBAGE

Symplocarpus foetidus (L.) Salisb. ex Nutt.

This unusual species still persists where it was planted in the WPA bog. Illustrated on the right is the early spathe, as it emerges in late January, along with the robust, erect rhizome bearing a big cluster of roots. In the center is a mature leathery spathe, surrounded by furled green leaves. On the left, a spathe has been stripped away to reveal the young compound fruit, which has formed on the globose spadix. The leaves, which resemble leaves of chard, produce a skunklike odor when bruised.

ONE-FLOWERED CANCER-ROOT
Orobanche uniflora L.

Lizard's Tail

Saururus cernuus L.

Found in the wet ravine bottoms of Lee Park, this plant derives its name from the Greek "sauros" (lizard) and "oura" (tail) and the Latin "cernuus" (nodding). It has a zigzag stem with drooping spikes of white flowers, which have no petals or sepals. Bessie Marshall captured the glaucousness on the underside of its heart-shaped leaves.

B.N.Marshall

Species in the Lee Park Herbarium
Collection Not Represented by Watercolors

Many of the 325 dried specimens in the Lee Park Herbarium Collection are not accompanied by watercolors. Some of these unpaired specimens are duplicates of species already represented by watercolors in the collection, but the seventy-three listed below represent species not illustrated in any of the watercolors.

Alum-Root, *Heuchera americana* L.

Arrow-Leaved Violet, *Viola sagittata* Ait.

Beech-Drops, *Epifagus virginiana* (L.) W. Bart.

Bellwort, *Uvularia puberula* Michx.

Black Haw, *Viburnum prunifolium* L.

Black Locust, *Robinia pseudo-acacia* L.

Blue-Stemmed Goldenrod, *Solidago caesia* L.

Boneset, *Eupatorium perfoliatum* L. var. *perfoliatum*

Bugle-Weed, *Lycopus virginicus* L.

Butterfly-Pea, *Clitoria mariana* L.

Cardinal-Flower, *Lobelia cardinalis* L.

Carolina Elephant's Foot, *Elephantopus carolinianus* Raeusch.

Cinquefoil, *Potentilla recta* L.

Common Bellwort, *Uvularia perfoliata* L.

Common Blue Wood Aster, *Aster cordifolius* L.

Common St. John's-Wort, *Hypericum perforatum* L.

Cornel-Leaved Aster, *Aster infirmus* Michx.

Cowbane, *Oxypolis rigidior* (L.) Raf.

Crested Fringed Orchis, *Platanthera cristata* (Michx.) R. Br.

Dittany, *Cunila origanoides* (L.) Britt.

False Dandelion, *Pyrrhopappus carolinianus* (Walt.) DC.

Flat-Topped Goldenrod, *Euthamia graminifolia* (L.) Nutt.

Fringed Loosestrife, *Lysimachia ciliata* L.

Grass-Leaved Golden Aster, *Pityopsis graminifolia* (Michx.) Nutt.

Ground-Cherry, *Physalis virginiana* Miller

Hairy Snoutbean, *Rhynchosia tomentosa* (L.) Hook. & Arn.

Heart-Leaved Alexanders, *Zizia aptera* (Gray) Fernald

Hercules' Club, *Aralia spinosa* L.

Hoary Tick-Trefoil, *Desmodium canescens* (L.) DC.

Horse-Mint, *Monarda punctata* L.

Indian Pipe, *Monotropa uniflora* L.

Lady's Thumb, *Polygonum persicaria* L.

Larger Withe-Rod, *Viburnum nudum* L.

Late Purple Aster, *Aster patens* Ait.

Lion's Foot, *Prenanthes serpentaria* Pursh

Loosely-Flowered Goat's Rue, *Tephrosia spicata* (Walt.) Torr. & Gray

Male-Berry, *Lyonia ligustrina* (L.) DC.

Mist-Flower, *Conoclinium coelestinum* (L.) DC.

Monkey-Flower, *Mimulus alatus* Ait.

Moth-Mullein, *Verbascum blattaria* L.

Naked-Flowered Tick-Trefoil, *Desmodium nudiflorum* (L.) DC.

New York Ironweed, *Vernonia noveboracensis* (L.) Michx.

Nodding Ladies' Tresses, *Spiranthes cernua* (L.) L.C. Rich.

Orange Coneflower, *Rudbeckia fulgida* Ait.

Ovate-Leaved Violet, *Viola sagittata* Ait. var. *ovata* (Nutt.) Torr. & Gray

Pale-Leaved Sunflower, *Helianthus strumosus* L.

Plantain-Leaved Everlasting or Pussytoes, *Antennaria plantaginifolia*
    (L.) Richardson

Prince's Feather, *Polygonum orientale* L.

Purple False Foxglove, *Agalinis purpurea* (L.) Pennell

Round-Leaved Thoroughwort, *Eupatorium rotundifolium* L.

Running Cedar or Running Pine, *Diphasiastrum digitatum* (Dill. ex
A. Braun) Holub

Rusty Black Haw, *Viburnum rufidulum* Raf.

Sensitive Pea, *Chamaecrista nictitans* (L.) Moench

Slender Aster, *Aster gracilis* Nutt.

Slender Bush-Clover, *Lespedeza virginica* (L.) Britt.

Slender Flat-Topped Goldenrod, *Euthamia tenuifolia* (Pursh) Nutt.

Slender Ladies' Tresses, *Spiranthes lacera* (Raf.) Raf.

Small-Flowered Agrimony, *Agrimonia parviflora* Ait.

Smooth Beard-Tongue, *Penstemon laevigata* Ait.

Southern Lobelia, *Lobelia georgiana* McVaugh

Spiderwort, *Tradescantia virginiana* L.

Starry Campion, *Silene stellata* (L.) Ait. f.

Striped Gentian, *Gentiana villosa* L.

Sweet Everlasting, *Gnaphalium obtusifolium* L.

Thimbleweed, *Anemone virginiana* L.

Virginia-Thistle, *Cirsium virginianum* (L.) Michx.

Virginia Willow, *Itea virginica* L.

Water-Hemlock, *Cicuta maculata* L.

Water-Pennywort, *Hydrocotyle umbellata* L.

Water-Plantain, *Alisma subcordatum* Raf.

Wax-Goldenweed, *Haplopappus ciliatus* (Nutt.) DC.

White Thoroughwort, *Eupatorium album* L.

Wild Pink, *Silene caroliniana* Walt.

Yellow Jessamine, *Gelsemium sempervirens* St. Hil.

INDEX OF PLANTS ILLUSTRATED

Italicized page numbers refer to illustrations

Cypripedium parviflorum var. pubescens, 252
Cytisus scoparius, 119

dangleberry, 160, 161
Daucus carota, 148
day-flower, common, 151
day-lily, 40, 156, 157
deerberry, 162, 163
dewberry, 2, 98, 155
Dianthus armeria, 158
Dioscorea villosa, 215
Diospyros virginiana, 208
dogwood, flowering, 2, 38, 52, 210, 211

elder, common, 219, 225
Elephantopus tomentosus, 120
elephant's foot, 120
Epigaea repens, 168, 169
Erigeron pulchellus, 181
Eryngium yuccifolium, 172, 173
Erythronium umbilicatum, 262
Euonymus americanus, 164
Eupatorium fistulosum, 231
Eupatorium hyssopifolium, 140
Euphorbia corollata, 132
everlasting, 181

false asphodel, 79, 241
false foxglove, blunt-leaved, 119
false foxglove, downy, 198
false foxglove, fern-leaved, 79, 199
fetterbush, swamp-, 251
feverfew, American, 97, 102
five-finger, 38, 130
flag, blue, 2, 16, 228
flag, slender blue, 229
Fragaria virginiana 98, 99
fringe-tree, 248

galax, 182, 183
Galax urceolata, 182, 183
Galearis spectabilis, 189
Gaylussacia baccata, 162
Gaylussacia dumosa, 160, 161
Gaylussacia frondosa, 160, 161
gentian, 265
gentian, coastal plain, 265
gentian, soapwort-, 265
Gentiana catesbaei, 265
Gentiana saponaria, 265
Gentiana sp., 265

Geranium maculatum, 266
ginger, Virginia wild, 49, 64, 174
goat's rue, 113
golden aster, Maryland, 117
golden-knee, 198
Goodyera pubescens, 192
grass-pink, 79, 237
green-and-gold, 198
greenbrier, glaucous-leaved, 153
greenbrier, laurel-leaved, 64, 245, 259

Hamamelis virginiana, 167
hawthorn, 206
hazel-nut, 41, 166
heal-all, 151
Helianthus angustifolius, 244
Helianthus atrorubens, 204
Hemerocallis fulva, 156, 157
hepatica, 182
Hepatica americana, 182
Hexastylis virginica, 174
Hieracium venosum, 197
holly, American, 212, 213
honeysuckle, Japanese, 61, 67, 78, 219, 245, 258
honeysuckle, trumpet-, 202
houstonia, large, 214
Houstonia caerulea, 134, 135
Houstonia purpurea, 214
huckleberry, black, 2, 43, 162
huckleberry, dwarf, 160, 161
hydrangea, wild, 168
Hydrangea arborescens, 168
Hypericum crux-andreae, 131
Hypericum gentianoides, 138
Hypericum hypericoides, 143
Hypoxis hirsuta, 135

Ilex opaca, 212, 213
Ilex verticillata, 247
Impatiens capensis, 220, 221
Indian hemp, 142, 143
Indian-physic, 79, 186, 187
indigo, wild, 196
indigo, yellow, 196
Ionactis linariifolius, 111
ipecac, false, 186, 187
Ipomoea hederacea, 126, 127
Ipomoea lacunosa, 125
Ipomoea pandurata, 128, 129
Ipomoea purpurea, 124, 125, 127

iris, dwarf, 101
Iris prismatica, 229
Iris verna, 101
Iris virginica, 228, 229
Isotria medeoloides, 5, 190
Isotria verticillata, 191

jack-in-the-pulpit, 41, 49, 264, 265
Jamestown lily, 254
joe-pye weed, 2, 40, 219, 231
Judas tree, 209

Kalmia latifolia, 170, 171
knotweed, Pennsylvania, 232

Lachnocaulon anceps, 239
ladies' tresses, linear-leaved, 64, 67, 235
lady's-slipper, larger yellow, 65, 252
lady's-slipper, pink, 17, 159, 193
lady's-slipper, stemless, 193
laurel, mountain, 41, 49, 159, 170, 171
leather-flower, silky, 8, 213
leopard's-bane, 41, 65, 107
Lespedeza repens, 132
Leucothoe racemosa, 251
Liatris spicata, 109
Liatris squarrosa, 79, 114
Lilium michauxii, 200, 201
Lilium superbum, 255
lily, Carolina-, 40, 42, 79, 200, 201
lily, turk's-cap, 2, 255
Lindera benzoin, 249
Liparis liliifolia, 253
Liriodendron tulipifera, 3, 210
liver leaf, 182
lizard's tail, 49, 270
lobelia, downy, 112
lobelia, great, 233
lobelia, nuttall's, 233
Lobelia nuttallii, 233
Lobelia puberula, 112
Lobelia siphilitica, 233
Lonicera japonica, 258
Lonicera sempervirens, 202
loosestrife, whorled, 201
lupine, wild, 38, 201
Lupinus perennis, 201
Lyonia mariana, 165
Lysimachia quadrifolia, 201

magnolia, laurel-, 28, 245, 257

snakeroot, small-leaved white, *187*

spice-bush, *249*

Spiranthes vernalis, 235

spleenwort, ebony-, *217*

spring-beauty, *42, 266, 267*

spurge, flowering, *132*

squarehead, *79, 213*

squaw-weed, Small's, *105*

staggerbush, *165*

star-grass, *135*

Stellaria media, 179

Stellaria pubera, 179

strawberry, wild, *98, 99*

strawberry-bush, *40, 164*

Strophostyles umbellata, 137

Stylosanthes biflora, 133

sundrops, *116*

sundrops, narrow-leaved, *116*

sunflower, hairy wood, *204*

sunflower, narrow-leaved, *244*

sunflower, purple-disk, *204*

sweet bay, *257*

Symphoricarpos orbiculatus, 149

Symplocarpus foetidus, 268, 269

Tephrosia virginiana, 113

Tetragonotheca helianthoides, 213

Thalictrum thalictroides, 176

Thaspium barbinode, 184

thistle, field-, *120, 121*

thorn, dwarf, *165*

thoroughwort, hyssop-leaved, *140*

tickseed, whorled, *196*

Tipularia discolor, 192

Tofieldia racemosa, 241

touch-me-not, spotted, *49, 219, 220, 221*

trumpet-creeper, *147*

trumpets, *16, 24, 75, 76, 79, 242, 243*

tulip-tree, *3, 49, 159, 210, 245*

turtlehead, *245, 261*

twayblade, *2, 253*

Typha latifolia, 223

Uvularia sessilifolia, 216

Vaccinium caesariense, 160, 161

Vaccinium formosum, 160, 161

Vaccinium fuscatum, 160, 161

Vaccinium pallidum, 160, 161

Vaccinium stamineum, 162, 163

Vaccinium tenellum, 79, 162

Verbascum thapsus, 150

vetch, Carolina, *205*

vetch, pale, *205*

Vicia caroliniana, 205

Vinca minor, 203

Viola bicolor, 140, 141

Viola pedata, 100

Viola primulifolia, 263

Viola sororia, 127

violet, bird's-foot, *97, 100*

violet, dog-tooth, *262*

violet, primrose-leaved, *263*

violet, woolly blue, *127*

willow, prairie, *41, 115*

winterberry, *247*

wintergreen, spotted, *172*

witch-hazel, *2, 167*

wood-sorrel, violet, *152*

wood-sorrel, yellow, *152*

Xanthorhiza simplicissima, 246

Xyris difformis var. *difformis, 243*

yam, wild, *215*

yellow-eyed grass, *243*

yellow-root, shrub, *245, 246*

Zephyranthes atamasca, 254

GENERAL INDEX